A Student Workbook for Public Speaking

A Student Workbook for Public Speaking

Speak From the Heart

Deanna L. Fassett
San José State University

Keith Nainby
California State University, Stanislaus

$SAGE

Los Angeles | London | New Delhi
Singapore | Washington DC

Los Angeles | London | New Delhi
Singapore | Washington DC

FOR INFORMATION:

SAGE Publications, Inc.
2455 Teller Road
Thousand Oaks, California 91320
E-mail: order@sagepub.com

SAGE Publications Ltd.
1 Oliver's Yard
55 City Road
London, EC1Y 1SP
United Kingdom

SAGE Publications India Pvt. Ltd.
B 1/I 1 Mohan Cooperative Industrial Area
Mathura Road, New Delhi 110 044
India

SAGE Publications Asia-Pacific Pte. Ltd.
3 Church Street
#10-04 Samsung Hub
Singapore 049483

Acquisitions Editor: Matthew Byrnie
Associate Editor: Nancy Loh
Editorial Assistant: Gabrielle Piccininni
Production Editor: Olivia Weber-Stenis
Copy Editor: Megan Granger
Typesetter: C&M Digitals (P) Ltd.
Proofreader: Eleni-Maria Georgiou
Cover Designer: Karine Hovsepian
Marketing Manager: Liz Thornton

Printed in the United States of America

ISBN 978-1-4522-9951-8

This book is printed on acid-free paper.

SFI label applies to text stock

13 14 15 16 17 10 9 8 7 6 5 4 3 2 1

Contents

How to Use This Book   vii

1. Introduction: What Does It Mean to Speak From the Heart?   1

2. Public Speaking Contexts   5

3. Topic Selection   9

4. Audience Analysis and Adaptation   13

5. Credibility and Ethical Communication   17

6. Thesis Statements   25

7. Organizing and Outlining Your Ideas   31

8. Transitions   37

9. Introductions   41

10. Attracting and Retaining Listeners' Interest   45

11. Compassionate Criticism   49

12. Language and Power   55

13. Evidence: Support for Your Main Ideas   59

14. Reasoning   65

15. Conclusions   73

16. Presentational Aids   77

17. Practice   81

18. Delivering Your Speech   87

19. Reflection and Self-Assessment   91

How to Use This Book

We invite you to *use* this book. We hope that you'll work through the exercises to practice your skills, deepen your understanding of public communication, and engage in self-reflection.

The 19 brief chapters of this workbook are designed to cover all the essential skills of public speaking, including selecting a topic, researching your topic, organizing your topic, overcoming speech anxiety, and delivering informative, persuasive, and special-occasion speeches. Each chapter includes a concise introduction to the most important skills and concepts related to each chapter topic, and offers opportunities for critical reflection on how to use each aspect of public speaking appropriately and effectively. Each chapter is paired with an activity, checklist, or worksheet that you may use to develop speeches, assess your progress, and chart your growth in becoming an effective public speaker.

Your instructor may ask you to write your responses to the questions in the workbook exercises directly in the text and to submit exercise pages as homework. You'll be able to tear the pages out easily along the perforations in the margin, and the three-hole punch format will allow you to store those pages in a binder if you wish. Each exercise is numbered (e.g., Exercise 17C) so you may also respond to the questions separately if you'd rather not write directly in the book or tear out the pages. Be sure to ask your instructor if you have any questions about specific assignments.

CHAPTER 1

Introduction

What Does It Mean to Speak From the Heart?

Communication is powerful. We may think of communication as a tool to transmit our thoughts and ideas to others. Understanding communication as a tool helps us feel in control, as though we can learn to wield communication effectively to express ourselves and persuade others. But there is also a more influential, less tangible quality to communication: It has the ability to create and transform. Communication does not only represent objects, ideas, and people in the world; it also gives rise to our understandings of the world and ourselves.

Take, for example, the language we use on a day-to-day basis to describe females. We might call them *women* or *girls*, *ladies* or *bitches*. While we might say that each of these terms refers to or describes women, it is important to note that each term, by carrying within it connotative meanings or associations, and historical relationships, also shapes our relationships with one another. The first term situates women and men as equals, while the others do not. Further, each term opens some doors and closes others in our understanding of the world. As Toni Morrison (1994), recipient of the Nobel Prize in Literature, observed: "Oppressive language does more than represent violence; it is violence; does more than represent the limits of knowledge; it limits knowledge" (p. 16). Morrison's insight speaks to the power of communication to transform our worlds toward constraint or possibility. Our communication does not simply name what is; it also gives rise to what might be.

Every time we speak, we affirm our sense of the world and encourage others to do the same. This challenges us to consider very carefully our communication choices. What do our words assert? If we imagine our communication as breathing life into the world, then apathy—a lack of care and regard for others and ourselves, for ideas and their implications—is a real danger. From a practical standpoint, we must fight apathy in our choice of subjects to discuss, our attention to source material to strengthen and nuance our ideas, our efforts to listen to others' ideas (especially when we find what they are saying confusing or offensive), and our sustained engagement with ideas over time. Speaking from the heart resists apathy, insisting on mindful awareness and purposeful engagement. As Brazilian educator and activist Paulo Freire (1992/2004) observed, "Changing language is part of the process of changing the world" (p. 56). To do so, we must be mindful of our communication. This reflection makes possible our ability to transform our lives and others' for the better.

Speaking from the heart is more than sharing heartfelt sentiment with our listeners, though it may include that as well. We tend to think of speaking from the heart as feeling moved to speak when we are overcome with emotion, as when we give a toast at a friend's wedding or eulogize a loved one or shout across a crowd at a protest. Emotions are an inextricable part of powerful communication, and our willingness to honor them will help us engage others—as long as we can remain attentive to the possibility that others might not feel exactly as we do. But there is more to speaking from the heart than responding to our emotions; it also means speaking with conviction and courage, caring enough about our communication and its implications in the world to do it well. Education scholar Parker Palmer (2011) helps us understand the heart as the space where what we know about the world, in all the ways we might know it, joins our own sense of passion and purpose.

> "Heart" comes from the Latin *cor* and points not merely to our emotions but to the core of the self, that center place where all of our ways of knowing converge—intellectual, emotional, sensory, intuitive, imaginative, experiential, relational, and bodily, among others. The heart is where we integrate what we know in our minds with what we know in our bones, the place where our knowledge can become more fully human. *Cor* is also the Latin root from which we get the word *courage*. When all that we understand of self and world comes together in the center place called the heart, we are more likely to find the courage to act humanely on what we know. (Palmer, 2011, p. 6)

Speaking from the heart means taking your communication seriously because it changes you and the others around you, for better or for worse. Your heart may function as a moral compass that challenges you to take risks, educate yourself in rich and substantive ways, and "act humanely" in the world.

Speaking from the heart is engaging in dialogic public speaking. For many of us, the idea of dialogic public speaking seems like an oxymoron, a contradiction. When we think of dialogues, we typically think of friends sitting together, listening intently and problem solving whole-heartedly. Yet, when we think of public speaking, most of us imagine politicians on the Senate floor or entertainers accepting awards—occasions where a solitary figure, often standing at a lectern, speaks over and across an audience. Communication professors have long argued that effective public speaking is really just an enlarged conversation (Winans, 1915). We could look at this cynically, in that whatever challenges you face as a speaker in an ordinary conversation will be enlarged in public speaking. However, we prefer to look at this hopefully, in that you likely already do many things well in conversation with others, and you can draw on these same qualities and skills when you speak in public.

Take, for example, a recent conversation you had with someone—a friend, family member, coworker, or even an acquaintance. How did you feel about communication in that moment? Did you feel heard? If there was a misunderstanding, were you able to address it? Not every conversation functions perfectly; in fact, we would venture to guess that most conversations are full of both success and frustration (and the more important the conversation, perhaps the more aware we are of this). That said, conversations involve the kind of back-and-forth speaking and listening we typically associate with dialogue. We can share an idea, hear it mirrored back for us, make adjustments, ask questions, offer examples, and so on—all in a fairly fluid exchange. In fact, some educators feel that conversation is a powerful means of learning; through conversation, peers can build knowledge together (Bruffee, 1993). Dialogic public speaking exemplifies collaborative learning, too.

To better understand what dialogic public speaking is, it may help to consider what makes a dialogue or dialogic communication special. Dialogue is characterized by a commitment to mutuality—the idea that learning occurs in sustained engagement with another, such that participants remain aware of and attentive to how they formed their own stances while also taking seriously others' perspectives (Spano, 2001). Practically speaking, dialogic public speaking is the opposite of monologic public speaking; instead of stating their position without regard for listeners, dialogic public speakers strive to engage with listeners, even (and perhaps especially) across what may be profound ideological differences. Our commitment to dialogic public speaking informs what we will share with you in this workbook, from how to select a topic to how to cite your sources—and all points in between.

We aim, through this workbook, to help you acquire insight about public speaking so you can rise to this challenge, to speak from the heart. In the pages that follow, we will offer what we know about public communication in hopes that you can put this information to good use. Though we have organized this information as you might need it for the development of a particular speech, remember that communication, as a process, is both idiosyncratic and recursive. In other words, please feel welcome to navigate the topics in this workbook as they suit you and your unique creative process. Please also remember that, though we discuss principles of meaningful public speaking, you may apply what you learn here to many different forms of public communication, including the messages you share outside of the classroom—in social groups and organizations, in the workplace, and through online social networks such as Facebook, Twitter, and Tumblr. We hope that the exercises help not only strengthen your skills but also encourage you to put them to good use. We hope you speak from your heart.

References

Bruffee, K. A. (1993). *Collaborative learning: Higher education, interdependence, and the authority of knowledge.* Baltimore, MD: Johns Hopkins University Press.

Freire, P. (2004). *Pedagogy of hope.* London: Continuum. (Original work published in 1992)

Morrison, T. (1994). *The Nobel lecture in literature, 1993.* New York: Knopf.

Palmer, P. (2011). *Healing the heart of democracy: The courage to create a politics worthy of the human spirit.* San Francisco: Jossey-Bass.

Spano, S. (2001). *Public dialogue and participatory democracy: The Cupertino Project.* Creskill, NJ: Hampton Press.

Winans, J. A. (1915). *Public speaking: Principles and practice.* Ithaca, NY: Sewell.

CHAPTER 2
Public Speaking Contexts

Public speaking textbooks often identify distinct "types" of public speeches. You will likely encounter these in your public speaking course: in your textbook, as part of the syllabus of topics/units for discussion, as names of assignments, or in some combination of these three ways. Our emphasis on speaking as dialogic means that we treat speaking as a process that deeply involves both speakers—such as students completing a specific assignment with detailed guidelines to earn a high grade—*and* listeners. These listeners may readily appear as students in captive classroom audiences, but they are also much more complex people for whom "captive classroom audience member" is only one role they are playing while listening. These listeners, because they have lived and are continuing to live beyond the limited context of your single speaking assignment, will bring their own passions, prejudices, and yes, even purposes, with them as they take their seats in the classroom. By doing so, they (re)shape the speaking context in ways that go beyond your assignment's designation of a certain speaking situation (e.g., a ceremony such as a funeral, where speakers deliver eulogies in a situation rhetorical scholars call "epideictic") or a certain speaking purpose (such as a "demonstration" speech, a common assignment in public speaking courses). For these reasons, we will explore in this section contexts for public speaking, acknowledging commonly used lists of speaking "types" while also complicating these lists and showing how you can speak more effectively by broadening your grasp of the context to include considerations beyond an assigned "situation" or "purpose."

The most common speech assignments you are likely to encounter in your course are related not to speaking "situations" but to speaking "purposes." These include the demonstration speech, the informative speech, and the persuasive speech. When we consider them from the perspective of dialogic public speaking, these purpose-centered speeches can be readily distinguished from one another based on the way each one brings you, the speaker, into a specific, evolving relationship with your audience.

A *demonstration* speaker encounters an audience that includes at least some novices who cannot perform, in a particular way, a task in which the speaker is more expert at the start of the speech. After an effective demonstration speech, the speaker and the novices in the audience will have moved closer together as a result of completing the task together. This task should be complex for two reasons: First, the task should be suitable for a stand-alone speech, a task that requires careful ordering of steps and reasons for success. Second, the task should be compelling enough that novices in the audience can understand *why* it is worth learning, because unmotivated learners who have not committed themselves to accomplishing the task for their own good reasons are difficult to teach.

An *informative* speaker encounters an audience that includes at least some listeners who, at the start of the speech, know less than the speaker about a topic that interests the entire community. Your central purpose in such a speech, then, is to educate your audience by providing them with carefully researched and effectively presented new information that will significantly broaden their understanding of your topic. Again, as we described above, the topic of an informative speech should be compelling enough to sustain audience focus for the entire speech. This is why the most effective informative speeches are those that identify and carefully explore previously taken-for-granted or unexamined aspects of the lives of the community as a whole. The recruitment and training procedure of your on-campus club, such as a sorority or fraternity, is a weak candidate for an informative speech because those who are significantly interested in that club will have already acknowledged themselves as "interested" in most cases, with the rest of the audience consisting of the "uninterested." However, if your sorority was founded based on a common ethnic heritage or has adopted a specific charitable organization as the beneficiary of its fundraising events or has a policy prohibiting "hazing" activities, you could develop a strong informative speech by uncovering historical processes related to the formation and preservation of invitation-only organizations at colleges and universities. A speech that examines such organizations could, potentially, function dialogically, as in the case of a demonstration speech, by tracing how the members of your school community reflect a range of competing, influential perspectives that have shaped on-campus sororities—and that continue to shape them as you speak. An informative speech that uncovers previously taken-for-granted aspects of the world you share with your audience members invites that audience to consider their own relationship with your topic—how they have acted in relation to sororities, for example, and how their actions function within the broader community to affect others in an ongoing way.

A *persuasive* speaker encounters an audience that has, across most if not all of its members, an unfulfilled need. This need might be widely recognized, such as prolonging life by maintaining physical fitness, or it might be a need the speaker helps the audience uncover, such as using everyday language about sexual practices in a more inclusive way. From a dialogic perspective, an effective persuasive speech results in an audience that more widely, more readily acknowledges the need highlighted by the speaker—and, in this way, such a speech creates a world with more shared ground, a world in which speakers and audience members can act toward a common purpose.

For this reason, the most effective persuasive speeches are those that focus on urgent, socially significant issues. A speech persuading us to change our diet, for example, is weak because this change requires internal, personal choices made by individuals over a long period of time (even family meals are often planned and executed by only a couple of family members). A speech persuading us to purchase chocolate or coffee only when the product bears a fair-trade label, however, can promote audience members' acting in concert and with mutual responsibility when they head off for snacks after class or at break time, and can promote social action if students intervene by requesting changes to campus contracts with vendors.

The most important reason to consider each speech as operating within a unique *context*, rather than being made for a specific *purpose*, is that when we consider dialogic public speaking as only one part of a larger system of communication rather than a bounded, formal situation, we realize that purposes overlap: When engaged in public communication in all its modes and contexts, we typically inform *and* persuade at once, often by demonstrating a task for novices or participating in marked rhetorical situations.

Take, for instance, a common speech assignment in an introductory public speaking course: a self-introduction speech. This assignment includes a built-in purpose made evident just by its title. But it would also be categorized as a special kind of "epideictic" or "ceremonial" speech, or a "speech of occasion," if assessed by the usual typologies of "speaking situations." This might seem strange at first, because there is no single, ordinary ceremonial occasion in which a person introduces her or himself to a group of relative strangers over a fixed length of time, with the stage all to her or himself (except, perhaps, in a public speaking class). To explain its classification, this would be a "speech of occasion" or "epideictic" speech because in it, the speaker is characterizing a specific person (in this case, her or himself) as worthy of public praise or blame before the assembled audience members. Initially, we might notice that this framing of a distinctive speaking "situation" helps us understand the context and our ethical obligations as speakers, because we can recognize that we are speaking at least implicitly to our character when we introduce ourselves. We are not merely allowing others to get to know us but are defending ourselves as people of good character who deserve our audience members' good will. How? By making appropriate choices that fit with our understanding of our listeners' values—when we select a funny story to tell; when we use specific terms to refer to people, places, and ideas; when we confine our introduction to the time and preparedness expectations set for the class, showing respect for resources; when we speak highly enough of ourselves to encourage listeners to like and/or identify with us but not so highly that they perceive us as conceited; and so on.

But if we move away from the "epideictic" classification and explore the purpose of such a speech on a more dialogic level, we encounter deeper questions about the nature of a speech of self-introduction. When, indeed, do we have an extended platform of self-introduction all to ourselves, without interruption, apart from a classroom setting? In what contexts would we introduce ourselves to a group of near-strangers who share one or two experiences and a common context with us (similar to our listeners, who are other students in this particular class who will also complete this assignment)? How would we begin to uncover the implicit expectations others have, in such contexts, that constrain how much we should say, which stories are appropriate, how kind we should be to ourselves, how much we should tease ourselves, and so on?

One such public communication context might be a Facebook profile. Even if you choose to make your Facebook profile publically searchable and viewable, you can identify certain shared values and expectations among potential audience members: They will have Internet access (likely reasonably fast access if they can search for your name and get usable results); they will value the information available on Facebook; and they will know, upon receiving viewable results, that you have made this choice with your privacy settings (or at least that you are not concerned enough about your profile's privacy to have adjusted your settings from the Facebook defaults). Of course, in nearly all cases, those who view your Facebook profile will have done so for a purpose (or with your permission) and, thus, will share much more in common with you—such as a recent encounter, mutual friends, mutual interests, or mutual online communities such as Twitter or Pinterest. When you develop a Facebook profile, you are analyzing your audience in ways that parallel how you might develop a speech of self-introduction, searching for common ground in terms of humor, shared topics of interest, overlapping past experiences, and mutual reference points in popular and/or local culture.

Should you add Pitbull to your "Music" list? Obviously, we communicate aspects of our identity when we publically share our taste in music, but naming Pitbull as a favorite musician functions on more complex levels as well: Who will respond positively to it, and who won't? What messages might this choice communicate to Cuban Americans who view your page? What messages might it communicate to women who view your page? Why might Cuban Americans respond in a distinctive way to your listing of Pitbull as a favorite? Why might women respond in a distinctive way to this favorite? How might their responses reflect viewers' underlying beliefs and values? How might their responses reflect viewers' personal experiences and histories?

Questions such as these, which emerge when we consider the dialogic dimensions of communication—even when it is as apparently static and controllable as a Facebook profile—become even more important when we return to the subject of a self-introduction speech in a college classroom. Clearly, if how you present yourself to the semipublic Facebook community encourages you to explore potential responses among your audience, and the underlying values, beliefs, experiences, and histories that shape these responses, then when introducing yourself to the more public, less controllable group in your public speaking class, your speech choices become that much more significant—both in terms of the impact of your choices on audience members and in terms of the relationship of your choices to the unique *context* that shapes them—as you prepare and deliver your speech.

Exercise 2A

1. Think about an upcoming communication assignment: What would you say is the purpose or function of this communication?

_____

_____

_____

_____

_____

_____

_____

2. How would a particular topic or issue change in approach from one common purpose (demonstrative, informative, persuasive) to another?

_____

_____

_____

_____

_____

_____

_____

Remember that you can also find guidance on how to develop your speech's purpose and thesis using SpeechPlanner (speechplanner.sagepub.com).

CHAPTER 3

Topic Selection

It is impossible to choose an effective topic without first considering the speaking occasion—the reason why you have chosen to speak or been asked by someone to speak—and the audience for your speech. Giving a eulogy, with the purpose of drawing listeners together to memorialize a loved one and share their grief, is organized by a different purpose than, say, creating a YouTube video to help LGBTQ youth understand that their experiences of pain, stigma, and violence will change and perhaps improve as they get older. Still, the purpose of each of these speaking occasions probably seems sharp and clear to us, especially since they are both most likely voluntary. When we are intrinsically motivated to speak, when we speak in our own time and for our own reasons, we often better understand our purpose and audience and the relationship between the two. But determining our purpose for an assigned presentation can be more challenging, especially if we are speaking before a captive audience of our peers. For assigned speaking occasions, we may have to work somewhat harder to define a purpose and audience for ourselves.

Purpose, Audience, and Voice

An awareness of and willingness to explore purpose, audience, and voice can help us better select and refine topics for our public speeches, especially in what may feel like more contrived classroom settings. As Peter Elbow (1998) argued in *Writing With Power: Techniques for Mastering the Writing Process*, "You don't write *to* teachers, you write *for* them" (p. 220). This is true of public speaking assignments as well. In other words, your professor may have commissioned a particular speech from you, but she or he is not the ideal or only audience member for that speech; to develop a meaningful speech, you must determine your own purpose or reason for sharing this particular message with this particular group of listeners. You can sometimes take cues for the purpose of your speech from the assignment instructions—for example, you may need to teach your audience how to do something or persuade your listeners to take a particular action—but without a deeper consideration of your reasons for speaking and how what you say emerges from and helps give back to a group of listeners, your topic will fall short.

Considering our audience can help refine the purpose of a speech. Audience analysis can yield important insights about listeners' expectations of and attitudes toward particular topics. As Elbow (1998) reminds us, engaging our audience gives rise to "a kind of magnetic field which exerts an organizing or focusing force on our words" (p. 191). For example, if you think you would like to address stem cell research for a persuasive speech in class, it may help you to know whether your audience members have prior knowledge of the subject (if they are, for example, science majors) or whether they have already established strong opinions on the subject (for example, if they have fundamentalist religious beliefs). These insights will help you refine your argument by helping you anticipate and substantively address the real interests and reservations your listeners will bring to your ideas.

Addressing your audience members' expectations and reservations in respectful and thought-provoking ways entails careful reflection on your voice as a speaker. While we will address delivery elsewhere, here we mean your choice of words. Elbow (1998) is helpful again here, reminding us that it is our job to "put a hex on words or on readers" (p. 280). Putting a hex or spell on our listeners is an apt metaphor for the power of our words. Our most powerful and memorable public speakers—from the historic to the contemporary, from the scholarly to the entertaining—became so because they could choose their words well and for maximum effect. Once you know who you'll be addressing (and what about them most defines and refines your message) and why, then you can speak with them in ways that will help them feel more inclined to listen.

For example, if your professor asks you to give an informative speech to the class on a socially signifi-cant topic, you will begin by considering what social significance means—to your particular audience and to the public overall. Generally speaking, socially significant topics are those that are relevant to a diverse audience and can help them better understand themselves and their relationships with others (whether public officers, organizations, neighbors, family members, coworkers, strangers, or friends). You will likely be drawn to topics you find interesting or with which you already have some experience; this can help you enhance your credibility with your listeners. If you are a parent of a toddler, then perhaps you'll want to speak on how your state inspects and licenses day-care facilities. If you are an accomplished pianist, then perhaps you'll want to speak on how best to appreciate music. The more you know about your listeners, the better you can tailor your speech to them, making your message more relevant and useful. If the majority of your classmates are not parents yet, then you will have to find ways to make a discussion that most would assume affects primarily parents relevant to them (perhaps by having them consider the children—e.g., nieces and nephews—in their lives who do attend day care, or perhaps by exploring the way they fund such efforts through tax dollars). If you plan to discuss classical music appreciation, then it would be helpful to learn if the majority of your classmates are active in the underground music scene in your city; it may not change your topic, but it would likely change how you approach your topic.

Brainstorming

Brainstorming topic ideas is a sound place to begin. At first, you should try to generate potential topic ideas without much regard for their viability; this will help you build creative momentum.

Exercise 3A

To help you brainstorm, we'll ask you a series of questions. As you answer each, try to keep an open mind. Think of concepts and questions, people and places, processes and events.

1. To get started, take stock of any *experiences* that are special or unique to you (this may include your many years attending soccer camp, your service in the military, or even that your birthday falls on a leap year). What do you already do well and enjoy?

   _____

   _____

   _____

_____

_____

_____

_____

2. Now consider your *interests and commitments*. What would you say is the central issue facing your generation today? What topics in the media attract your interest (because you find them either fascinating or annoying)?

_____

_____

_____

_____

_____

_____

_____

_____

3. Now consider your *education*. What is your major? What is your minor? Have you learned skills or concepts in your coursework that you find especially important for others to know? List these here. What kinds of issues or challenges face people who work in the career(s) you'd like to pursue?

_____

_____

_____

_____

_____

_____

_____

4. Now consider the people you care about, your *friends and family*. Has anything happened to someone you care about that you think others should explore more fully? What kinds of issues and concerns matter most to them? Do you agree with them?

_____

_____

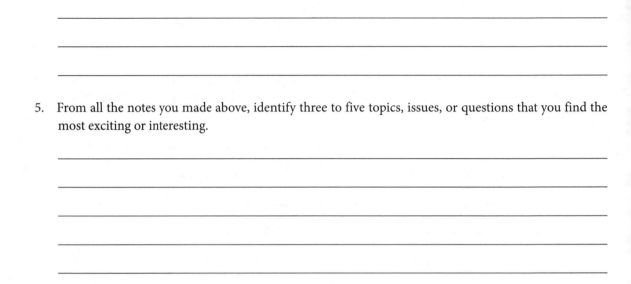

5. From all the notes you made above, identify three to five topics, issues, or questions that you find the most exciting or interesting.

_____

_____

_____

_____

_____

Have another look at each item on this list, and ask yourself the following questions: (1) Is this topic appropriate for this particular speaking occasion? (2) Do I have a personal connection to this topic? (3) Do I already have or can I develop expertise in this topic in the time I have available to prepare? If you can answer yes to all three of these questions, then your brainstorming has been fruitful; if not, then you can always start the process anew. By preparing well in advance, you leave yourself plenty of time to brainstorm and percolate on possible topics while checking your Twitter feed, watching television, or eating lunch with friends.

Reference

Elbow, P. (1998). *Writing with power: Techniques for mastering the writing process* (2nd ed.). New York: Oxford University Press.

Remember that you can also find guidance on how to select a speech topic in SpeechPlanner (speechplanner.sagepub.com).

CHAPTER 4

Audience Analysis and Adaptation

To better discern what arguments and evidence listeners will find meaningful and compelling, speakers can engage in audience analysis. This kind of analysis begins at the moment a speaker is invited (or assigned) to speak, continues into the speaking occasion itself, and even extends into reflection on whether the speaker achieved her or his goal(s). A careful exploration of the listeners' experiences, interests, and values can help a speaker not only develop an effective speech but also adapt her or his ideas to the particular exigencies of the speaking situation.

Analysis

A speaker's audience analysis often begins at the moment she or he is invited (or assigned) to speak. Even the question of what to discuss or why is often influenced by who is in the audience and the speaker's perceptions of those listeners. Learning all you reasonably can about an audience can help you make good decisions about how many ideas to address and in what order, what sources your listeners will find compelling, which examples will work best, and whether they already have strong attitudes and opinions regarding your topic.

If you have sought to speak to a particular organization, then you may already have an insider or otherwise knowledgeable understanding of what the members of that organization do. For example, you might choose to petition your local city council to add a stop sign in your neighborhood, or you might recruit new members for your fraternity or sorority during Frosh orientation. Similarly, if you have been invited to give a presentation (for example, because of your specialized expertise or experiences), you can often learn a lot about the organization by discussing it with the person who invited you to speak. In such cases, you can begin your analysis and speech development from what you already know about your audience.

If you are speaking for a captive audience, such as a room full of other students who are required to take an oral communication course as part of their general education curriculum, then audience analysis may still be helpful. Learning what you can about your peers will help you avoid assuming too much about what they already do and do not know, believe and do not believe about your subject. Even in a college classroom, where we might assume a certain degree of similarity in age or experience, there can still be considerable heterogeneity in experiences, interests, and values.

One way to learn about your audience is to make careful, provisional guesses about them based on their demographic characteristics. Demographic data help identify patterns in populations, for example, along age, ability, education level, ethnicity/race, geographic location, gender, income, language of origin, military status, nationality, political affiliation, religion, or sexual orientation. Knowing demographic data about your audience can help you tailor your approach, your examples, your sources, and your vocabulary; you may

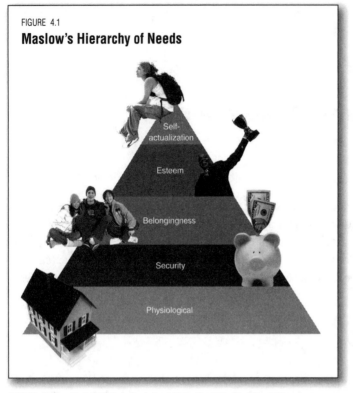

FIGURE 4.1
Maslow's Hierarchy of Needs

Self-actualization

Esteem

Belongingness

Security

Physiological

SOURCE: Abraham Maslow, *Toward a Psychology of Being,* New York: John Wiley, 1962.

foreground some experiences and ideas and background others. Once you know some basics about your audience, you can begin to infer their interest in, experiences with, and positions regarding your topic. Just take care to remember that these must be provisional and flexible guesses; as you're no doubt already aware, demographic data are not predictively certain, especially when it comes to complex issues and ideas.

Psychologist Abraham Maslow's hierarchy of needs can also help you make educated guesses about what your listeners will find compelling. Through studying motivation, Maslow (1943) identified a series of human needs he set in hierarchical relationship to one another. You can see a representation of the hierarchy in Figure 4.1 at left.

Maslow argued that all people (irrespective of demographic patterns) need to satisfy the needs at the base of the hierarchy, such as survival and security needs, before addressing higher-order needs, such as self-actualization. This can be helpful to remember as you develop your speech. Appealing to your listeners' need for safety, stability, or belonging (in an ethical, manipulation-free way) can help strengthen your own efforts at public communication.

Adaptation

Another kind of audience analysis occurs during the speech itself. Here, a speaker engages in mindful awareness of how her or his listeners are encountering the speaking occasion, including the speaker and the content of the speech. Some adaptations are fairly easy to anticipate, such as accommodating the audience's fatigue during an early Monday morning presentation or knowing that a recent news report will raise questions for them regarding your topic. But if you are carefully reading your audience members' verbal and nonverbal communication, then you have yet another opportunity to reach them with your words by adjusting your speech in the moment and on the fly.

Effective practice and delivery is integral to audience analysis. By scanning the room, you can quickly surmise whether the audience is supportive or hostile, confused or curious. By listening for whether audience members laugh or gasp at certain parts of your speech, you will develop a sense of how they are reacting to your ideas. At home, you developed your speech for an *imagined* audience, but in the moment, you are tailoring your speech for this *particular* audience. This necessitates being well-informed about your topic in general and your speech in particular; the more comfortable you are with your message, the more capable you will be of meeting your listeners' needs in the moment. What your listeners say and how they behave will help you strengthen your speech for them, giving you yet another chance to achieve your goal(s) as a speaker.

Exercise 4A

1. Consider an upcoming speaking opportunity and describe your audience in as much detail as you can. What demographic patterns can you discern? What provisional educated guesses can you make about their interest in, experiences with, and positions on your topic/argument?

    _____

    _____

    _____

    _____

    _____

    _____

    _____

2. Given the topic for your upcoming speech, how might you make the most of at least three of your audience members' needs, as identified by Maslow?

    _____

    _____

    _____

    _____

    _____

    _____

    _____

3. What kinds of adaptations have you found yourself making in the course of a speech?

    _____

    _____

    _____

    _____

_____

_____

_____

_____

4. Former President Bill Clinton is well-known for his skills as a public speaker. When he nominated President Barack Obama for reelection, he gave a speech that exemplified his skills in adaptation in particular. You can find a comparison of what Clinton wrote and what he eventually said on *The Atlantic Wire* website (Bennett, 2012). What lessons about adaptation can you take away for your own public speaking efforts?

_____

_____

_____

_____

_____

_____

_____

_____

References

Bennett, D. (2012, September 6). What Bill Clinton wrote vs. what Bill Clinton said. *Atlantic Wire*. Retrieved from http://www.theatlanticwire.com/politics/2012/09/what-bill-clinton-said-vs-what-he-wrote/56562/

Maslow, A. H. (1943). A theory of human motivation. *Psychological Review, 50,* 370–396.

Remember that you can also find guidance on audience analysis in SpeechPlanner (speechplanner.sagepub.com).

CHAPTER 5
Credibility and Ethical Communication

Exercise 5A

1. Take a moment and make a list of people you respect and admire.

_____

_____

_____

_____

_____

2. Why do you respect and admire them?

_____

_____

_____

_____

_____

Whether you were thinking of a public figure, such as a former president or popular musician, or someone much closer to you, such as a parent or mentor, chances are you respect and admire these people because you find them credible. *Credibility* is a term we use to describe how trustworthy a person is. Speakers cultivate this trust through multiple means: by being knowledgeable and sharing similarly trustworthy information in ethical ways, by living their lives in light of their principles, and by communicating their interest in and good will toward their listeners. In establishing credibility, you earn your right to your listeners' time.

You can help establish yourself as credible by showing that you are knowledgeable about your topic. It may help to think about how you might choose a surgeon. You would likely want someone who is credentialed, who has her or his MD from a highly regarded medical school. Furthermore, you would likely want someone who has performed the necessary procedure dozens or hundreds of times. As a speaker, you can communicate your expertise by having a candid conversation with your listeners about how you became interested in and knowledgeable about your topic. This conversation often entails sharing your qualifications—for example, any relevant coursework or professional experiences that help make you more knowledgeable about your topic. Showing your listeners that you've consulted credible sources as part of your research process also helps bolster your credibility; even if you do not have direct or extensive experience with a given topic, you can share insights from people who do. Remember, as a speaker, you are only as credible as the sources you choose to support your message.

You can help establish yourself as credible by living your life in a principled way—what we might think of as walking your talk or practicing what you preach. By consistently following your own beliefs and values, and by taking your own good advice, you demonstrate that you have integrity. We are perhaps most critical of our own parents' credibility on this front; any time a parent says, "Do as I say, not as I do," that parent harms her or his credibility. If someone tells you to buckle your seatbelt but fails to do so her or himself, it can be hard to take the message seriously. While expertise is important in choosing a surgeon, whether she or he has integrity matters, too. What if you were to learn that the surgeon falsified data in her or his research? Or what if you learned that the surgeon is in the middle of a protracted custody dispute amidst allegations of child abuse and neglect? That would likely influence the trust you feel in your surgeon, no matter her or his professional experience.

You can help establish yourself as credible by communicating your interest in and good will toward your listeners. In part, you achieve this through practiced, conversational delivery; when you are confident about your message and your performance, you can maintain consistent eye contact, engage in purposeful movement that complements your message, and interact with your audience in an engaging, compelling way. You also achieve this by choosing examples and words that communicate your care and regard for your listeners' well-being. If we stay with our surgeon example, we might think of this quality as "bedside manner." We are likely to be more reassured by surgeons who express concern for our well-being, who are interested in our concerns, who listen to us, and who take care in how they explain complicated and anxiety-producing procedures. This quality, in and of itself, would not matter more than a surgeon's (or speaker's) expertise, but it does still affect our perceptions of her or his credibility.

Exercise 5B

To consider how the different aspects of credibility work together, evaluate the credibility of a public figure (such as cyclist Lance Armstrong, singer Chris Brown, or former Secretary of State and First Lady Hillary Clinton).

1. List the name of the public figure you've selected, and how credibility is important to her or his role.

   _____

   _____

   _____

   _____

   _____

2. Where does this person struggle with credibility?

   _____

   _____

_____

_____

_____

3. Do you find her or him credible? Why or why not?

_____

_____

_____

_____

Academic Integrity and Research

Academic integrity refers to the cultural expectations we have for the people who build and share knowledge. Because academic environments such as colleges and universities are concerned with building relevant, meaningful, and accurate knowledge, a speaker's or writer's credibility is intertwined with academic integrity (sometimes described as academic honesty). All public communication has consequences, and speakers bear responsibility for making sure they are communicating with audiences in ways that improve, rather than harm, relationships and insight about the world. Establishing your interest in and good will toward your listeners is an important component of your credibility as a speaker, but to earn the right to suggest a change to your listeners' lives, you must also establish yourself as someone who is knowledgeable about your subject and ethical in how you conduct research about that subject. To embody academic integrity, speakers must consult appropriate sources, ethically share information from (and about) those sources, and provide accurate citation information for them. We'll address each of these in turn here. If you have specific questions about how to find particular sources in your college or university library, please consult a reference librarian at your school.

1. *Speakers must consult appropriate sources.* What counts as an appropriate source might vary a bit from one speaking occasion to another. For instance, the research and evidence you engage in as you prepare a wedding toast is different from what you would need to prepare an informative speech on the history of stem cell treatments. For the first, your personal experience with (that embarrassing or touching story about) the bride or groom is probably sufficient for your toast, but for the second, you will need to reference trustworthy research. Your research may come from newspapers, journals, or other periodicals; books; interviews; government documents; media texts (such as songs, television shows, films); or websites, blogs, or social media sites (such as Twitter, Tumblr, or Facebook). At a minimum, your sources must speak meaningfully to the issue or topic at hand, but there is more to choosing sources. An ethical speaker looks for the best research on her or his subject matter, reading with equal care and critique the research that both challenges and supports her or his position. Further, an ethical speaker also anticipates the audience's attitudes toward a given source, selecting material listeners will find trustworthy and valuable or helping them understand why material they are less likely to respect still may be worth their attention.

2. *Speakers must ethically share information from (and about) sources.* Because your own credibility evolves, at least in part, from the strength of your source material, it is important to choose that material wisely. To do so, you need to know enough about the author or organization—the source of your information—to evaluate her/his/its credibility. Is the author trustworthy? Does she or he have the expertise to support the claims she or he makes? You will likely need to share with your listeners some background information about your source so they will agree with you that this information is trustworthy and useful to your argument. For example, telling your listeners that the source for your information is "the Internet" or "Yahoo! News" tells your listeners little about the quality of the information (including, for example, the relevant expertise of the author—perhaps she is a Nobel Prize–winning physicist—or the biases of the organization that funded a particular research study—perhaps it is an environmental advocacy group funded by an oil company).

You will share information from your sources by either quoting them directly or paraphrasing from them. Generally speaking, if you can share information from a source without losing something important from the author's phrasing, you should paraphrase; however, if the author has unique or powerful wording, you should quote directly.

For example, let's say you're interested in exploring your university's decision to open a "portal" or satellite campus in another country and, as part of your research, you review an article from *The New York Times*: "Liberal Education in Authoritarian Places" by Jim Sleeper (2013). In this article, Sleeper raises concern over the way U.S. universities open campuses in other countries in such a way as to maximize enrollments and profits while paying little heed to how they must compromise ideals of academic freedom to accommodate restrictive government regimes. If you decide to share with your listeners that there are those who express concern over the ways universities are compromising their missions in entering arrangements with totalitarian governments, then you are paraphrasing. If, however, you are moved by one of Sleeper's specific statements, then you will likely quote him; for example,

> If you look past their soaring rhetoric, you'll see globe-trotting university presidents and trustees who are defining down their expectations of what a liberal education means, much as corporations do when they look the other way at shoddy labor and environmental practices abroad. The difference, of course, is that a university's mission is to question such arrangements, not to facilitate them. (Para. 7)

Your responsibility as a speaker extends to doing your best to learn whether this information is worth sharing with your listeners. As this is an opinion piece in *The New York Times*, it is worth noting whose opinion you're considering sharing. The article indicates that the author, Jim Sleeper, is a lecturer at Yale University, where there has been controversy about a partnership with National Singapore University (NSU). A quick Google search will give you access to his website, where you can find his biography as well as links to his published works. You can review this information to determine whether his position on global university partnerships is useful for your research or your listeners' understanding of the issues involved. Upon consideration, you may decide to quote him, or you may decide to use the information he shares about the Yale–NSU partnership to chase down other source material from the *Yale Daily News* or *The Chronicle of Higher Education*.

3. *Speakers must provide accurate citation information for sources.* You should clearly indicate any source material you use to strengthen your understanding of an issue or situation, specifically any material you use in developing your speech and speech outline. You should cite *each* source at least *four* times:

(1) aloud to your listeners, (2) in the text of your speech outline, (3) in the references or works cited page of your outline, and (4) on any visual aid that uses information from that source.

Part of how you establish credibility as a researcher is in citing your source material accurately and consistently. A number of professional organizations offer guidelines for how to cite sources, including the American Psychological Association (APA) and the Modern Language Association (MLA). You can learn more about source citation (as well as all sorts of useful writing topics, from grammar to punctuation) on the website for the Online Writing Lab at Purdue University (owl.english.purdue.edu/). Using source citation guidelines can help you include all the relevant information a listener (or reader) would need if she or he wanted to explore and evaluate the sources you used. If you are speaking in a particular class, it is wise to use the guidelines most closely associated with that discipline; if you are unsure which citation system to use, the course syllabus or professor will likely clarify.

Your selection of source material should be intentional, and you should carefully evaluate each source for its quality and usefulness in developing your public communication. By effectively documenting these sources and sharing them with your listeners in a consistent and helpful way, you will enhance your own credibility as a speaker. When your listeners perceive you to be credible and your conclusions to be formed from sound and ethical investigation, your words will have greater reach and impact.

Exercise 5C

1. What are three to five steps you can take as a public communicator to establish yourself as credible with the audience(s) you most want to reach?

_____

_____

_____

_____

_____

2. What kinds of publication outlets would your audience consider credible?

_____

_____

_____

_____

_____

_____

_____

_____

_____

3. Of the sources you're using for your next speech, which is the most credible? Which is the least credible?

_____

_____

_____

_____

_____

_____

_____

_____

4. Choose one of your sources for the upcoming speech.

   a. Create a bibliographic citation in APA or MLA style for your chosen source.

_____

_____

_____

_____

_____

_____

_____

_____

   b. Create an in-text citation in APA or MLA style for your chosen source.

_____

_____

_____

_____

_____

_____

_____

_____

c. Describe how the information in this source is useful to your speech.

_____

_____

_____

_____

_____

_____

_____

d. Describe any limitations of this source for your research.

_____

_____

_____

_____

_____

_____

_____

e. Describe why this is a credible source, as you would to your listeners.

_____

_____

_____

_____

_____

_____

_____

_____

Reference

Sleeper, J. (2013, August 31). Liberal education in authoritarian places. *New York Times.* Retrieved from http://www.nytimes.com/2013/09/01/opinion/sunday/liberal-education-in-authoritarian-places.html?pagewanted=all&_r=0

Remember that you can also find guidance on establishing credibility and citing your research sources in SpeechPlanner (speechplanner.sagepub.com).

CHAPTER 6
Thesis Statements

The primary purpose of a thesis statement within a public speech is somewhat different from its primary purpose in an essay (you likely first learned about thesis statements when learning about writing essays). When developing an effective speech, a thesis statement is important because when you create and modify it, you sharpen your focus and better understand *your own* ideas. Audience members need a thesis statement to help us organize what you say in your speech, but you will use other tools (evidence, repetition, presentational aids) to reinforce the thesis statement at multiple points. However, you cannot make these reinforcements useful to your audience unless you, the speaker, first prepare an effective thesis statement to organize your own ideas in relation to your audience members' potential range of knowledge, interests, and attitudes. The key elements of an effective thesis statement include the following:

1. An effective thesis statement is precise.
2. An effective thesis statement is unique.
3. An effective thesis statement is direct.
4. An effective thesis statement is argumentative, making an argument by showing *how* ideas are related to one another.

Let's discuss these in order, then practice developing an effective thesis statement.

Suppose you are creating a persuasive speech asking that your audience members contact an elected official and request more public funding for higher education (schooling beyond K–12). One step you need to take is to develop an effective thesis statement; following the list of key elements above, you might support your speech by developing an effective thesis statement like this one:

Public colleges and universities such as ours provide necessary access to higher education for students like Robin here in California, but recent funding trends limit this access; we should each write to Governor Brown and urge him to restore the state budget to the apportion levels of 2009–2010 so all qualified candidates will have the access we enjoy.

A thesis statement like this one is easiest to create by beginning with core ideas for the speech and then using the process we outline here to shape and reshape these ideas as you develop the speech in relation to your audience members and their needs. Here's one example of the process by which you might develop this thesis statement using the four key elements identified above.

Precise

Your thesis statement should be *precise* in identifying ideas and distinguishing them from other, similar ideas. If your speech is persuasive and you have to motivate audience members to take a specific action related to funding higher education, then asking them to write an elected official might be a good idea. However, notice that government money supports higher education in a variety of ways, such as through subsidizing student loans at many different kinds of colleges and universities, funding grants and other special programs at many different kinds of colleges and universities, and partially subsidizing (lowering the cost of tuition and fees) attendance at state-sponsored (public) colleges and universities.

For these reasons, your thesis statement should be precise about which forms of government funding you want your audience members to advocate. Noun phrases such as "higher ed" or "public support" are tempting to use because they are simple and easy to follow, but in a thesis statement your listeners should hear only about the specific type of additional funding you believe is currently needed (more loans? more grants? more enrollment in public schools?). Also, a persuasive speech should be precise about what, exactly, audience members can immediately do to help meet that need (write a letter? make a phone call? to whom, asking for what?). When your thesis statement is precise enough to name which form of additional funding you want to increase, and also what your audience can do to help make that happen, you have the foundation for an effective thesis.

Exercise 6A

1. Try starting a thesis statement with *precise* noun phrases, using the ideas for your next speech.

_____

_____

_____

_____

_____

_____

_____

Unique

Your thesis statement should be *unique* in offering ideas that relate to you, your audience, and your evidence. A good test for an effective thesis: If anyone else in your class could use the exact same thesis for this speaking assignment, then your thesis needs to be tweaked to differentiate your speech from any other. Your audience analysis, for instance, might suggest to you a good approach in your speech about increasing public support for higher education, if you attend a public community college with much more affordable fees than competing private colleges. You might decide to center your claims on "public colleges and universities such as ours" as the best way for the state to support higher education. Striving for precision, you might identify the governor of your state as an official whose political platform emphasizes support for higher education, deciding to name him in your speech and suggesting a letter-writing campaign to his office.

But as you research statistical evidence for your speech, suppose you realize that the simplest way to illustrate why some students need lower-cost degree programs is to trace the family, income, and goals of one imaginary student as an example (this is a wise approach for an oral context because listeners always need help making numbers—which are abstract—more concrete, through ideas such as income and personal goals). Give your example student a name, like Robin (a fun one because it is gender neutral and suggests flight, a poetic way to highlight the freedom a degree can provide). Notice that by combining your audience analysis (local details relevant to your community) with an example of your own invention (Robin), you have developed a unique approach to your topic—one that would be subtly different from even the speech of another member of your class.

Exercise 6B

1. Try adding to your thesis statement with *unique* noun phrases, using the ideas for your next speech.

_____

_____

_____

_____

_____

_____

_____

Direct

Your thesis statement should be *direct* in offering only those ideas that are absolutely necessary for making your speech understood. Those precise and unique noun phrases we have already explored should be subjects in your thesis statement, and they should be followed by strong action verbs that are not qualified or nuanced. Qualifications and nuances are important in public speaking because you want to assure your audience that you are credible (not bending the truth by omitting relevant evidence or offering fallacies as conclusions) and that your claims are well considered (most topics worth exploring in a public speech will have multiple intelligent perspectives associated with them). However, the thesis statement is not the time to acknowledge and examine these subtleties; they should be uncovered during the body of the speech, as you discuss evidence.

For these reasons, our sample persuasive speech about state funding in higher education might include action verbs such as *provide* (something money does when given to those who need it), *limit* (something money does when access is taken away from those who need it), and *increase* (something an elected official can do with regard to money within a budget allocation). You should use present-tense action verbs because they imply specific relationships; avoid using forms of "to be" (*is, was, will be*) and participial phrases ("has limited") because these dull the argument in your thesis statement. In our example, we want to write a phrase that includes *limit* as an action verb; writing that "inadequate state support has limited student access" is weak. Notice, for instance, that if we write simply "state support has limited," the meaning is ambiguous: Is *limited* a verb, something that state support has *done*, or is it an adjective, as in "state support has limited value"? Especially when we plan to deliver our final thesis statement in an oral/aural setting, we want to use language that avoids ambiguous phrasing and that listeners can parse easily. Using present-tense action verbs in your thesis statement, a vital element of your speech, helps you practice effective language use.

As you develop your speech over time, your thesis statement can help guide your search for evidence (e.g., how much of an increase in funding, specifically, should I advocate, and why?). Your thesis statement can be modified later to fit the work you have done. Suppose you found that, in fact, state funding for schools such as yours had actually decreased over the 2-year period immediately preceding the time of your speech. For instance, according to *The Daily Californian*—the independent student newspaper at UC Berkeley—California's spending on public higher education decreased a total of 13.5% from the fiscal year that ended in 2010 to the fiscal year that ended in 2012 (Applegate, 2012). If you offered this information as part of the evidence in your speech, you might use the action verb *restore* in place of *increase* within your final thesis statement.

Exercise 6C

1. Try adding action verbs to your thesis statement using the ideas for your next speech.

_____

_____

_____

_____

_____

_____

_____

Argumentative

Your thesis statement should *make an argument* in just one (or at most, two) declarative sentences. This should be the core argument of your speech and should show how the ideas in the thesis statement are related to one another in one specific, contingent way that leads to the conclusion you want your audience to reach as they listen to your speech. In a persuasive speech, your assignment will often require you to call for an immediate action, as in our example of writing a letter to a state governor. But all types of speeches urge audience members to reach a conclusion (e.g., "I can now make tamales myself"; "I agree that our former mayor deserves to be honored for her leadership during a distinctive time of civic crisis"; "I better understand the reasons some religious institutions are given tax-exempt status"). In an effective thesis statement, all ideas (all noun phrases) are linked together with strong action verbs that urge the audience to a single conclusion.

Working on your thesis statement in this way guides you, in your development of the speech as a whole, to ask a series of important questions: Which ideas in this speech do I make strong claims about, and how can I best support those claims in a direct way? Which ideas in this speech are controversial or might foster disagreement from my audience, and how can I best defend my claims in a direct way that also acknowledges these differences? These are, remember, qualifications and nuances; so, as we discussed in the third point above, they are relevant within the body of the speech rather than in the thesis statement. But now you can recognize how your development of an effective thesis statement is, first and foremost, for you: It helps you understand how to organize the work of creating the rest of the elements of your speech. As we have explored here, the thesis statement will evolve as you conduct research, sculpt evidence, and organize your claims. But it should evolve *with* your speech and serve as a framework, or scaffolding, for the speech, changing in shape as a scaffold changes with a new building—moving to one side or another, growing taller or shorter, but always giving you an understanding, from start to finish, of where you are heading and why.

Reference

Applegate, J. (2012, January 23). Study: State suffered dramatic drop in funding for higher education. *Daily Californian.* Retrieved from http://www.dailycal.org/2012/01/23/study-state-suffered-dramatic-drop-in-funding-for-higher-education/

Remember that you can also find guidance on preparing your thesis statement in SpeechPlanner (speechplanner.sagepub.com).

CHAPTER 7
Organizing and Outlining Your Ideas

You are likely already familiar with outlining as one means of structuring and strengthening your written work. We usually learn about outlining as a type of brainstorming, perhaps alongside free writing or concept mapping. Some people find it challenging to brainstorm effectively through outlining, choosing instead to make lists, draw, or otherwise represent their ideas more freely. Still, it's worth thinking about why teachers in general, and public speaking teachers in particular, emphasize the value of outlining.

Speaking and writing share similar qualities. Whether we are sharing a speech in public or preparing a blog entry, we are concerned with reaching our audience with our message in such a way that they will listen to it. As we addressed earlier, both speakers and writers are concerned with navigating purpose, audience, and voice. That said, oral communication is distinct because it is also emergent, unpredictable, and ephemeral. For example, a speech is emergent in that it responds to a particular speaking occasion and audience. Speakers often adjust their message to reflect the context in which they're speaking (for example, the day's headlines or whether the speech is at lunchtime or first thing in the morning); they also typically adapt to their audience's reactions (from yawns to questions) in the moment. A speech may be unpredictable in that, no matter how well prepared, a speaker cannot (and should not) assume that her or his speech will proceed exactly as planned. Hecklers can disrupt a speech, but so can an ill-timed leaf blower or the fact that the listeners are eagerly awaiting lunch. Finally, a speech is, above all, ephemeral in that the listeners typically witness it only once. Even if we could rewind the speech, as we might if we record it, there is no way to exactly re-create the experience in all its rich complexity. For example, we can watch and even reread the transcript of President Obama's speech immediately following the shootings at Sandy Hook Elementary School in December 2012, and we can feel moved by his words, but this experience and the power of the speech cannot be the same as they were in that moment. Because speeches are emergent, unpredictable, and ephemeral, it is crucial that we provide our listeners with clues to help them follow, remember, and make meaning of our talk.

By outlining, we can identify, consider, and adjust the structural components of our communication. This gives public speakers at least three advantages: First, we will be more likely to include the most common structural elements in our work (e.g., the different parts of an effective introduction, balance in coverage of more than one idea, transitions, etc.). Second, we will be better able to articulate and evaluate the relationship between main and supporting points in our arguments. Finally, by developing a more skeletal outline, instead of writing speeches word-for-word, speakers will be better able to prepare for a more extemporaneous or conversational delivery style.

Developing and Grouping Main Ideas

Outlines are, in a sense, the spine of your speech; they represent the structure of your ideas and how they build on one another. Knowing what information to share in your speech and how to share it can be challenging, especially if you're knowledgeable about and have direct personal experience with the subject. For example, demonstration speeches can be especially tricky: How many steps does it take to tie a necktie or make pad thai or request a change of grade from a professor? Any one of these could be 10 steps or 3. There is no set number of steps or main ideas in any speech topic; this is determined by each individual speaker, by the logic or reasoning used to organize her or his thoughts. However, it is important to remember that your listeners can track and digest only a limited amount of information. For this reason, most experienced public speakers address between two and five supporting points in a presentation.

Let's imagine that, for an informative speech assignment, you decide to teach your classmates what it's like to be a student athlete. Such a speech could help shape their understanding of and opinions about student athletes. You might, for instance, choose to refute stereotypes of student athletes, which could result in a lot of possible main points. Or you might choose to approach your speech as a day in the life of a student athlete, which could be organized into points by hours of the day or mealtimes. Or you might choose to structure your speech according to the advantages and disadvantages associated with being a student athlete, which incorporate those other possible approaches in a simple, memorable way.

Strong main points are like topic sentences: Each one represents a distinct support of your argument or focus. As such, you would phrase a main point as a single declarative sentence, rather than as a question or paragraph.

Outlining Format

The two most common formal outlines for public speeches, at least in public speaking classes, are full-sentence outlines and presentational or "keyword" outlines (more on presentational outlines below). The first of these, the full-sentence outline, begins as a working outline, usually a collection of your thoughts in response to the key components of your speech. It becomes formal through your use of alphanumerically ordered complete sentences showing hierarchical coordination and subordination of ideas. You have probably already seen this outline format:

I. Main Point 1

    A. Supporting Point 1
       1. Evidence 1
       2. Evidence 2

    B. Supporting Point 2
       1. Evidence 1
       2. Evidence 2

Transition

II. Main Point 2

    A. Supporting Point 1
       1. Evidence 1
       2. Evidence 2

    B. Supporting Point 2
       1. Evidence 1
       2. Evidence 2

    C. Supporting Point 3
       1. Evidence 1
       2. Evidence 2

The structure for your own outline will vary depending on the purpose and function of your speech, the number of main points, the kind and quality of your evidence, and other contextual factors. Effective formatting will help you identify and strengthen your two to five main points by making sure they are relatively equal in importance, mutually exclusive, and parallel in construction.

Coordination and Subordination

The use of Roman numeral formatting might seem arbitrary, and to some extent it is, but it is important as a technique that helps speakers determine whether we have (1) effectively limited ourselves to two to five discrete main ideas, (2) developed ideas of relatively equal importance and value, and (3) marshaled enough evidence for each of those ideas. Coordination, making sure comparable ideas appear parallel in the outline, and subordination, signaling which ideas are larger or more significant to your argument than others, guide the development of an outline.

Returning to the example of the speech on student athletes, it may help to see examples of stronger and weaker coordination:

Stronger:	*Weaker:*
I. Student athletes receive a number of benefits for their participation in collegiate sports. II. Student athletes also face challenges as a result of their dual role.	I. There are many different kinds of student athletes. II. Student athletes receive benefits. III. Student athletes face challenges. IV. Football players must deal with stereotypes.

What makes the second outline weaker is that the main points are not discrete. There is overlap between Points III and IV. Further, the four ideas are not parallel in importance or wording. Remember, too, it is easier for you and your listeners to remember that you will address two ideas in your speech, compared with four ideas.

Here are examples of stronger and weaker subordination:

Stronger:	*Weaker:*

I. Student athletes receive a number of benefits for their participation in collegiate sports.
   A. They receive health-related advantages.
     1. They receive health care.
     2. They can consult with trainers and nutritionists.
   B. They receive learning-related advantages.
     1. They have access to tutors.
     2. They receive priority registration.
	I. Student athletes receive a number of benefits for their participation in collegiate sports.
	   A. They can consult nutritionists.
	   B. They can register early for classes.
	   C. The football team gets to travel to Hawaii.
	   D. They have access to tutors.

Here, again, the second outline is weaker because the four supporting points are not parallel in scope and importance. Further, it would be easier for a listener to remember that there are two or three types of benefits associated with being a student athlete, instead of four specific benefits. Effective coordination and subordination within an outline challenge you as a speaker to understand why you've chosen these particular ideas and not others, as well as the logic that connects one idea to the next. Making the spine of your speech more transparent in this way helps you take better ownership of not just what you are sharing but how you share it. This helps you better accomplish your goals as a speaker because not only are you more likely to engage your listeners in a conversational way, but they will better remember and use what you have said.

Organizational Patterns

While you may choose to develop your outline organically from your own ideas as they occur to you, you might also find it helpful or reassuring to know that there are common organizational patterns for speeches. You might choose to organize your thoughts *chronologically* (for example, by sharing events related to your topic by seasons in the year), *spatially* or geographically (for example, by introducing your ideas directionally, as you would in providing an overview or following the contours of a map), or *sequentially* (for example, by sharing with listeners the steps in a process).

For informative or persuasive speeches, where you will likely share ideas that are controversial and multiperspectival, you might consider choosing an organizational pattern that helps you illuminate the causes of and responses to your given issue. These include *compare–contrast, cause–effect, advantage–disadvantage* (the design for our student athlete speech), and *problem–solution*. Bearing these patterns in mind, you can choose a structure for your speech outline that helps you better organize your thoughts and share them in a memorable way with your listeners.

Of particular use for persuasive speakers is an organizational pattern called *Monroe's Motivated Sequence (MMS)*. Unlike problem–solution design, MMS challenges a speaker to concretely address the effects of her or his proposal. There are five steps to MMS: attention, need, satisfaction, visualization, and action. These are as they sound: (1) In the *attention* step, you draw in your listeners and help them see the relevance of your speech; (2) in the *need* step, you help your listeners understand that they have a need your speech can address (in a sense, you establish that they face a problem they should care about and to which you have a solution); (3) in the *satisfaction* step, you show your listeners how you can meet their need (or, in other words, how you have a means of solving the problem they face); (4) in the *visualization* step, you help your listeners visualize or imagine how their lives will be affected by either adopting or rejecting your solution (i.e., how their lives will be improved by following or harmed by not following your recommendations); and, finally, (5) in the *action* step, you challenge your listeners to take measures to achieve your solution. By following this five-step process, you stand a better chance of effectively convincing your listeners.

The Keyword Outline

The presentational or keyword outline is, as it sounds, a brief outline or listing of keywords that will help you remember what you meant to say next in your speech if you falter or forget. It is unwise to deliver your speech from a full-sentence outline because this would likely harm your delivery. You would be tempted, especially if you experience public speaking anxiety, to read word-for-word from this outline, diminishing your credibility with your listeners. It would be better to talk through your full-sentence outline until you feel comfortable with the content and organization of your speech. As you practice from this developed outline, your goal is not to memorize specific wording but to become comfortable with the ideas of your speech and the logic that binds them together. You can then create a keyword outline that includes only the barest of information to keep you on track. Your keyword outline might look as simple as the following:

AG: Impressions of student athletes?

Cred: 3 years of NCAA Div 1 football

T: Today I hope to help you better understand the benefits and challenges associated with being a student athlete.

P: Benefits and challenges

     I.   Benefits

         A. Health

         B. Academic

    II. Challenges

         A. Demands on time

         B. Stereotypes

Review points and restate thesis.

C: Instead of the negative stereotypes you've heard (ref their initial impressions), I hope you imagine student athletes as not only healthy but scholarly.

Outlining brings to mind abstract, decontextualized exercises. But the more simple and memorable you can make the structure of your speech, the easier it will be for you and your listeners to remember. Following the simple steps we include here will help you better learn and share the information from your speech with your listeners, helping you achieve your goals as a speaker. Without an appropriately simple and logical structure, your efforts as a public speaker will suffer—at best, you may still entertain or share a bit of information with your listeners, but at worst, you may waste their time or permanently and negatively alter their impressions of you and your message. Try giving some time and attention to the relationships between your ideas so you can better achieve your goals as a speaker.

Exercise 7A

1. What are the main points for your next speech?

_____

_____

_____

_____

_____

_____

_____

_____

_____

2. Evaluate your main points. Are they mutually exclusive? (In other words, is each point a single, coherent idea, with no overlap with other ideas?) Using effective coordination and subordination, order these points in light of a structure (e.g., chronology, cause–effect, MMS) that will help you and your listeners better remember the information you share.

_____

_____

_____

_____

_____

_____

_____

_____

Remember that you can also practice outlining your speeches in SpeechPlanner (speechplanner.sagepub.com).

CHAPTER 8

Transitions

As you have likely practiced for years already when writing essays, creating effective transitions helps your audience understand how *you* believe your ideas fit with one another. As we have explored in this workbook, communication of any kind can be described as "making an argument," even when there is no dispute or persuasion immediately evident, because all communication (1) names a state of affairs in the world (explicitly) and (2) helps bring about a relationship of that current state of affairs to a possible future (implicitly) by focusing on particular ideas rather than others, by speaking to some audiences rather than others, and by speaking in particular ways (word choice, tone, and so on) rather than others.

Structure

Since all communication makes an argument, transitions between ideas are vital ways your audience can grasp the logic of your argument—why you have chosen this focus at this time in this place for this audience. Transitions do so by accomplishing some structural tasks (i.e., they *structure* your argument when you speak):

1. Transitions order ideas.

2. Transitions identify causes and their effects.

3. Transitions give reasons for a speaker's claims.

Let's explore these structural tasks one at a time using the example of our speech about restoring support for state colleges and universities.

1. Transitions *order* ideas by reinforcing the sequence in which audience members encounter those ideas in your speech. "Ordering" can refer to two different kinds of priority: "first things first" priority (such as counting main points through the speech) and "more important than other things" priority (such as showing how one point cannot be true unless another one is also true). In our example speech, suppose the first main point we develop is the rationale for public funding beyond the high school level. An effective transition from our introduction to this first main point might be as follows:

> To establish my rationale for advocating state support, I will now explain why state governments got involved in higher education in the first place, by tracing the historical arguments about how states have both an economic and an ethical interest in ensuring access to higher education.

Notice that this transition includes *both* kinds of ordering of ideas: It deals with historical context prior to dealing with the present budget ("first things first"), and it deals with historical agreements that must have been made prior to dealing with the details of how best to live up to those agreements ("more important than other things"). It has another advantage as well: It serves as a mini-preview of this point in our speech, which audience members now know will touch on both economic and ethical discussions.

Not all transitions in your own speech must do both kinds of ordering at once; sometimes, your sequence of main points does not involve the "importance" kind of priority. But even when all you are doing in a transition is ordering ideas in a simple sequence ("first, second, third"), you should always acknowledge this sequence and keep it consistent. You always have *some* reason for arranging your main points in the order you do (see the unit on organizational patterns in Chapter 8), and your transitions structure your speech by acknowledging this sequence. You can sometimes do this explicitly by using language that *enumerates* the sequence of ideas in your speech—using words such as "one trend" or "the second issue" when writing your transitions. But you can also do this implicitly just by carefully attending to how you arrange the noun phrases in your transitions. Notice that our example transition includes the phrase, "both an economic and an ethical interest"; this suggests that the speaker will treat economic interest first in this main point and ethical interest second. The speaker needs to address them in this order or needs to reword the transition to match the plan for the speech. We will return to the role of audience expectation later in this unit.

2. Transitions identify *causes* and their effects when stitching ideas together, using phrasing that reflects these cause–effect relationships. Returning to our example transition:

> To establish my rationale for advocating state support, I will now explain why state governments got involved in higher education in the first place, by tracing the historical arguments about how states have both an economic and an ethical interest in ensuring access to higher education.

This transition indicates a specific cause–effect relationship: States currently fund higher education at some level because of arguments about economic and ethical interests. Not all your transitions will do this, depending on your speech, and as you can see from Chapter 8 of this workbook, not all speeches are explicitly based on large-scale, cause-and-effect relationships. But part of the task of an effective transition is to show these kinds of cause–effect relationships among your ideas, even when the connections are subtle. If you are having trouble creating a transition within your speech, try asking what cause–effect relationships your ideas reveal.

3. Transitions give *reasons* for a speaker's claims. Returning again to our example transition, the opening phrase, "to establish my rationale for advocating state support," lets audience members know that the upcoming material has a specific purpose within the framework of the speech. This is easy to recognize in the context of a persuasive speech such as our example, but it applies equally to all public speaking contexts. If this were a speech in which informative or ceremonial purposes were more important than persuasion, for instance, changes in language could reflect that distinct purpose without losing the structural function of reason giving. The opening phrase could, instead, read like this, without changing the rest of the transition: "to help you understand the foundations of public higher education" (for an informative speech) or "to recognize the motivations that led us to devote ourselves to public higher education" (for a ceremonial speech).

Credibility in an Oral/Aural Context

Developing effective transitions becomes an especially important goal in a public speaking context, for two additional reasons beyond merely guiding listeners through the logic of your argument. First, in such a context, listeners cannot "go back" as they can when reading an essay. If listeners find themselves lost or confused, strong transitions that accomplish the structural functions we discussed can reorient them. This is why transitions usually restate, in subtly different language, what has just been covered and what will be covered next. In our example transition, the phrase "advocating state support" likely restates something just described in the preceding introduction: that the speaker wants the audience to take action to promote state support for higher education. Similarly, the phrase "tracing historical arguments" likely summarizes the type of material about to be presented. Notice that if transitions are delivered with confidence, as written, with appropriate variation in vocal tone and tempo (see the unit on delivery in Chapter 18), listeners who get lost in either the introduction or, more likely, the details of the following main point, can rely on a transition to keep them on track within the speech as a whole.

This "keeping listeners on track with transitions" effort relates to the second unique feature of transitions in an oral/aural context: You can show your listeners respect for their needs in this context (remember, they can't "go back") and demonstrate your own commitment to their active role in the dialogic process by creating and delivering strong transitions. In other words, more than any other element of your speech—more than an introduction or conclusion, more than supporting evidence appropriately cited, more even than a lively presentational aid—strong transitions establish and maintain your credibility as a speaker. Think of yourself as a kind of tour guide, such as the kind found in state or national parks (often rangers) or museums (often docents), or on tours in private settings (e.g., popular attractions). This person's subject knowledge (of natural features, of the area, and so on) and personality are both important, without question, but we would contend that if this person does not consistently demonstrate a confident grasp of what will happen next and why, and communicate this grasp to the audience, then subject knowledge and personality cannot rescue the audience's experience. When speaking, your transitions are your opportunity to demonstrate consistently that you are the *only* reliable "tour guide" to your own speech, so use these transitions as your best evidence of powerful credibility.

SpeechPlanner

Sp

Remember that you can also find guidance on using transitions in SpeechPlanner (speechplanner.sagepub.com).

CHAPTER 9

Introductions

First impressions are undeniably important. While they may not totally determine the outcome of a relationship, whether on a first date or with a gathered audience, they do shape how others read and interpret your communication, making it easier or harder for you to be heard and taken seriously. Think a moment about the most recent time you met someone for the first time: What did you think? What did you notice about her or his communication? Did you find yourself drawn to (or uninterested in) this person? What else influenced your impression of her or him? Did a friend introduce this person to you? Did you run into each other by chance? Introductions are exciting because they give rise to possibilities. Introductions help create meaningful and sometimes lasting relationships, and that is true in the public speaking context as well. A well-crafted introduction draws in your listeners, establishes you as a credible voice on your topic, implicates your listeners in your goal(s) as a speaker, and provides both you and your listeners with a structure to navigate the speech. We'll address each of these four components here.

1. *A well-crafted introduction draws in your listeners.* Who would make a more positive impression for you—someone who expresses an interest in you (your background, interests, and needs) or someone who seems to be beginning a conversation that has little to do with you? Beginning your speech with attention-getting opening material is important to affirm and extend the dialogue you hope to have with your audience. We often casually refer to this opening material as the attention-getter, but it is important to remember that it may be more than a single sentence (for example, it could be a story). Effective attention-getters establish or reaffirm a connection between speaker, audience, and topic. These can include humorous anecdotes and startling statistics, rhetorical questions, or brief discussions—as long as you have chosen material that is consistent with your purpose for the speech and appropriate for your audience.

Let's return to our speech asking listeners to urge California's Governor Brown to reestablish adequate funding to public colleges and universities. You may have a witty cartoon image of the state of public higher education you can share at the start, or you could open with a discussion with your listeners about what they take to be the purpose and meaning of higher education. You could also open with a startling statistic that affects someone, either hypothetical or real, helping your listeners find themselves in what may feel like a complex and institutional topic. For example:

> I think most of us are pretty thankful for this opportunity to be in college, right? Even when we're tired and beat up at finals, we know that getting a college degree will make a difference in our own and our families' lives. Robin, for instance, whose family is working class going back many generations, has worked hard to achieve qualifying grades for college but has not earned the grades or standardized test scores that a private university would respond to with a large scholarship award. Robin needs to earn more money than just enough to live as a student because the family needs

additional financial support; so any school Robin chooses must be within close driving distance of home. How can Robin earn an accredited degree without access to a local, affordable state college? According to a study by the American Institutes for Research and Nexus Research and Policy Center, earning that bachelor's degree will net you between 300,000 and 550,000 in additional income in comparison with someone who has earned only a high school diploma (Adams, 2011, para. 9). That's a lot of money—and just imagine what you can do if you save or invest it! But as taxpayers and state governments reduce funding for public colleges and universities, fewer people will have access to the opportunities we now enjoy.

2. *A well-crafted introduction establishes you as a credible voice on your topic.* Your audience members need to know why they should listen to you; explaining how you are knowledgeable and trustworthy on a subject helps reassure them of your intentions and invites them to engage fully in your ideas. While you will demonstrate your credibility during a speech in a variety of ways, from citing your sources to projecting confidence and goodwill, you should also explicitly address your credibility in the introduction of your speech by explaining how you became interested in and knowledgeable about your topic.

For example:

I became interested in this subject when I took a social foundations of education class last semester. In that class, we learned about the history of the American educational system as an imperfect but still important means of upward mobility. To learn more about the effects of reduced funding on student access, I interviewed my professor in that class, and I also researched government policy reports, national publications such as *The Chronicle of Higher Education*, and our own local and campus newspapers.

3. *A well-crafted introduction implicates your listeners in your goal(s) as a speaker.* As a speaker, you will need to provide your listeners with a clear sense of your goal(s) for the speech; we described this earlier as a thesis statement (see Chapter 6). You should state in your introduction what you hope your listeners will think, feel, know, or do at the conclusion of your speech. In other words, this is not only your goal(s) for the speech but a reflection of what you feel your listeners' relationship to the speech's goal(s) should be. By showing them that they affect and are affected by your topic, you implicate them in the speech—you help them understand that they must pay attention because they are already or should become involved.

Our earlier example is a strong thesis because it not only states the speaker's intention or goal for the speech but also how listeners are affected by, and therefore implicated in, the issue.

Public colleges and universities like ours provide necessary access to higher education for students like Robin here in California, but recent funding trends limit this access; we should each write to Governor Brown and urge him to restore the state budget to the apportion levels of 2009–2010 so all qualified candidates will have the access we enjoy.

4. *A well-crafted introduction provides both you and your listeners with a structure for navigating the speech.* Because listeners will likely hear your speech only once, it is important that you provide them with as many clues as possible regarding how you will support your ideas. Often, speakers refer to this as a preview, in that we forecast the structure and scope of what will occur in the speech. The preview often follows the thesis and provides an overview of the two to five main points you will address during your speech. In a persuasive speech, the preview would likely forecast the reasons why your argument is sound.

For example:

Today, we'll be discussing three points: First, we'll review the benefits of a college education and why affordable access is so important; second, we'll look at Governor Brown's higher education appropriation decisions and their effects on who is and is not able to attend college; and, finally, we'll see how restoring the state budget to 2009–2010 apportion levels will make higher education a reality for more students like Robin.

Exercise 9A

Now it's your turn. Try to develop your introduction for an upcoming presentation here, taking care to address each of these four components:

1. Share something attention-getting with respect to your topic.

_____

_____

_____

_____

_____

_____

_____

2. Establish yourself as credible.

_____

_____

_____

_____

_____

_____

3. Share your thesis, explaining to your audience how they are implicated in your goal(s).

_____

_____

_____

_____

_____

_____

_____

4. Preview the two to five main ideas that will support your thesis.

_____

_____

_____

_____

_____

_____

_____

Reference

Adams, C. (2011, May 11). Study chronicles financial benefits of bachelor's degree. *Education Week*. Retrieved from http://blogs.edweek.org/edweek/college_bound/2011/05/study_chronicles_financial_benefits_of_a_bachelors_degree.html

Remember that you can find additional guidance on crafting introductions in SpeechPlanner (speechplanner.sagepub.com).

CHAPTER 10

Attracting and Retaining Listeners' Interest

In hopes of being integrative (at best—and repetitive, at worst), we would like to address how to attract and retain your listeners' interest. As you're no doubt already well aware, public speaking is a one-time event; in most instances, you have only one chance to achieve your goal(s) as a speaker. Your words will effect some action in the world—though the question remains, will that action be positive or negative? Will you motivate and excite your listeners? Will you help them improve their lives? Or will you generate disinterest and apathy?

Exercise 10A

1. We find reflecting on past teachers a helpful way to think about "being interesting." What have teachers in your past done to discourage your interest in a given subject or skill?

   _____

   _____

   _____

   _____

   _____

   _____

2. Perhaps those teachers were dispassionate about their subjects, or unprepared, disorganized, or hostile to your questions and experiences. Now let's think about the teachers who were effective in taking a complex topic or skill and making it interesting, relevant, and achievable for you. How did they do it?

   _____

   _____

   _____

   _____

_____

_____

_____

Generally speaking, good teachers and good public speakers have a lot in common. They are well prepared and well organized; they communicate, both verbally and nonverbally, their interest in and passion for the subject, as well as their interest in how you, the listener, can use that information; and they not only elicit feedback but also take that input seriously.

Preparedness is essential for most purposeful and effective public speaking. This means beginning preparations well in advance of the date you are scheduled to speak. By starting early, you honor yourself with time and respect; you take yourself seriously enough to care about what you say to your audience and how you say it. You give yourself space to care about what your communication does in the world. Preparedness entails engaging in audience analysis, developing an appropriate thesis that draws in and implicates or challenges your listeners in some way (that essentially demands their attention), identifying a limited number of supporting points and supporting them with credible sources, and, finally, practicing your speech so you can speak *with* your listeners instead of *at* them. Remember, there are many qualities people find engaging that you can consider using as you develop your speech—for example, surprise, humor, sincerity and honesty, suspense, and immediacy.

Communicating your passion for an argument, issue, or subject is essential to attracting and retaining your listeners' interest. If they do not believe you care about your topic, then they have no real reason to listen to it themselves. Often, speakers do care about their topics, but because of a lack of preparation and practice, they fail to perform that interest and excitement in ways their listeners can experience; this speaks to the importance of preparedness again. Verbally, speakers can communicate their passion for their ideas by signaling their credibility as speakers, using descriptive vocabulary, asking audience members questions and engaging them in discussion about their experiences with those ideas, and establishing the relevance of their ideas for their listeners' lives. Nonverbally, speakers can establish and maintain eye contact, speak with emotion, and move throughout the space and gesture purposefully, closing the literal and figurative distance between themselves and their listeners.

Finally, good teachers and good speakers both elicit feedback from their listeners. They not only scan the room to see whether people are paying attention, but they also welcome questions, invite perspectives and experiences, and, when appropriate, ask for suggestions. Speakers who know how to attract and maintain their listeners' interest recognize that public speaking is more dialogic than monologic and that meeting their goal(s) as speakers is a collaborative adventure.

Exercise 10B

1. What are three to five steps you can take to attract your listeners' interest during your next speech?

_____

_____

_____

_____

_____

_____

_____

2. What are three to five steps you can take to retain your listeners' interest during your next speech?

_____

_____

_____

_____

_____

_____

_____

CHAPTER 11

Compassionate Criticism

One consequence of recognizing that public speaking is dialogic—even if its dialogic character is not immediately obvious—is the attention this draws to our mutual responsibility for one another as speakers and listeners. This includes some of the ideas we have already explored in this workbook, such as the importance of your audience members' values, needs, and attitudes when establishing credibility, or the importance of identifying socially significant issues when choosing a topic. Yet we describe public speaking as dialogic for one reason above any other in our writing here: In a dialogic frame, we can appreciate that the impact of a single public speech always extends in time to the past and the future, as well as the present. Effective public speaking necessarily emerges from a particular speaker's vision and a particular audience's past experiences and sociocultural situations; in the same way, effective public speaking, by highlighting one person's (the speaker's) specific vision of the world, brings speaker and audience into closer contact with a possible future. This is true not only of persuasive speeches that call for action but of all forms of public speaking. Even in an informal speaking moment—such as a homemade YouTube clip—when we engage in public communication, we urge our audience to grasp what we grasp about the current state of affairs and to respond to it in particular ways.

Exercise 11A

1. Choose a single YouTube clip that you find compelling, and describe in your own words how this clip *encourages* certain kinds of responses from viewers.

    _____

    _____

    _____

    _____

    _____

    _____

2. Now, using that same YouTube clip, describe in your own words how this clip *discourages* certain kinds of responses from viewers.

This means that public speaking always demands a response from the audience, even when that demand is implicit rather than explicit. Responses themselves are what make dialogic communication different from communication framed monologically (as isolated messages that are distinct from one another). Responses, then, have their own ethical and social weight, and we have our own obligations as audience members:

- To respect the ideas of public speakers
- To listen with care as they speak
- To evaluate their claims with seriousness
- To treat their speaking efforts with compassion

Notice that we sometimes meet these obligations in *how* we attend to the speech itself while we listen; we sometimes meet them afterward, in either formal (assigned) or informal responses; and we sometimes meet them in how we, as individuals, choose to engage the community affected by the speech. Each of these obligations stems from the dialogic frame, which indicates a relationship between *compassion* and *criticism*:

- We should strive, as audience members, for a *compassionate* relationship with public speakers because we want to ensure that the speaker's communication creates a mutually responsive community, one that acknowledges us and our importance to the community. We help create that community, along with the speaker, by choosing to engage the speaker, with care for her or his feelings and by believing that she or he has good intentions for our community.

- We should strive, as audience members, for a *critical* (not "negative" but "shaped by critique") relationship with public speakers because we want to hold the speaker accountable for the potential consequences of her or his communication for our community and because we want the speaker, like the community as a whole, to grow in a positive way. We help create that community of growth, along with the speaker, by choosing to engage the speaker as if her or his ideas and presentation have importance for the community and, therefore, require our deliberate attention and response so the speaker's communication can improve over time.

Compassion

Sometimes, compassion comes to us easily as audience members because we find ourselves sharing the perspective of a public speaker; the ideas seem self-evidently important, and the speaker's characterization of the world matches our own. However, responding with compassion in other situations, those in which the speaker's worldview diverges from our own, requires commitment and practice.

The first step is to make compassion a priority in your response. Just as you probably learn best when your instructors treat your well-being as important, speakers can make sense of your responses only when you lead with compassion. Even when you disagree strongly with a speaker, you will find that if you respond with hostility or apathy, the speaker is unlikely to engage your response and continue the dialogue. To continue the dialogue, even contradictory ideas should be framed, in your response, as *possibilities* rather than *conclusions* so that you invite the speaker to consider your claims and actually *move* in terms of her or his perspective. Demands produce rigidity and inhibit dialogue, while invitations, in contrast, can produce movement and sustain dialogue.

Another helpful step, in addition to using a language of possibility when you respond to a speech, is to practice *empathy*. This means voluntarily adopting the perspective of the public speaker and imagining how you might engage the response you plan to offer. In the moment just after completing a speech for a grade, in front of peers who habitually judge qualities such as your intelligence and attractiveness, how would you feel emotionally? How open would you be to negative responses? The more often you practice empathy, imagining yourself in the other person's position, the easier it will be for you to lead with compassion when choosing your words and using your body to give emphasis to those words in your response to a public speech.

Exercise 11B

1. Describe a specific public speaking choice someone might make that would be *very* challenging for you, as an audience member, to respond to with compassion.

    _____

    _____

    _____

    _____

    _____

    _____

2. Now identify how you might develop a response that is *definitely* compassionate in addressing the challenging speaking choice you outlined above; this might involve

    ■ using compassionate language in direct response,

- providing supportive feedback (verbally or nonverbally) that establishes a bond of mutual respect (even if the speaker did not begin by showing respect), or
- taking specific action in discussion with the community affected by the speech:

_____

_____

_____

_____

_____

_____

_____

_____

_____

_____

_____

Criticism

Just as a public speaker's communication can and should improve over time in response to a community, an audience member's feedback skills can and should improve over time as well. You can help develop your skills as a critical respondent, one who helps public speakers grow and develop over time, by following these guidelines when offering feedback for a speech:

1. Be specific.
2. Be positive.
3. Give reasons.
4. Take responsibility.
5. Begin and end with strengths.

Let's discuss and practice these one by one. Please rewatch the YouTube clip you chose for Exercise 6A earlier in this unit; you will use this clip again in the next exercises.

1. Be *specific* rather than vague. Returning to our example of the speech about restoring support for affordable state colleges and universities, suppose you find, as an audience member, that the speaker spends too much time developing the example of a hypothetical student, Robin, and that this material is unhelpful; you believe that the precious public speaking time devoted to Robin could be put to better use, perhaps by explaining the challenges involved in state budgets. A vague, unhelpful response might be, "Your speech was distracting because you focused on random examples you just made up." A more specific, helpful response might be, "The example of Robin was not necessary."

2. Be *positive* about possibilities for growth rather than negative and backward-looking. A negative, unhelpful response might be, "Why did you make up that student Robin as an example?" A positive, helpful response might be, "Next time, how can you use more real-life, one-sentence examples with greater variety?"

3. Give *reasons* for each suggestion you offer so speakers can better grasp the foundation of your feedback. An unfounded, unhelpful response might be, "We don't need to hear about fake people to understand why state schools are important." A reason-based, helpful response might be, "Given that your listeners in the classroom are enrolled in a state school, we probably already understand the life circumstances that lead a person to choose one. We might be better motivated by learning about new ideas, perhaps more about the state budgets."

4. Take *responsibility* when you choose the words for your feedback. An evasive, unhelpful response might be, "Who's going to care about someone you just made up?" A helpful response grounded in responsibility might be, "I found it hard to care about Robin's chances to go to school once I realized this was not a real person."

5. Begin and end with *strengths* from the speech. This is especially important when you offer extended feedback, such as in a peer evaluation essay assignment. But you can also practice this when offering just a single response, such as in this example: "I really liked how you tried to make us care about human beings in your speech, since then we weren't just looking at numbers. The Robin example took a lot of time, though, and I think you can use that time to give other concrete examples, maybe from the state budget and how actual people are affected by it. I hope you keep using concrete examples like these in your next speech."

Exercise 11C

1. Return now to the YouTube clip you chose for Exercise 11A, and practice writing a sample response to it. Assess your response by asking if all five of the effective approaches to criticism helped shape it.

_____

_____

_____

_____

_____

_____

_____

_____

_____

_____

_____

_____

_____

_____

CHAPTER 12

Language and Power

When we conceive of our public speaking audience members as people engaged in dialogue with us, we can more easily recognize our responsibility to use our own speaking resources—our language, our research, our physical presence—in ways that respect and acknowledge those audience members' expectations of us. Reverse the positions in a public speaking situation, imagining yourself as an audience member: How could a speaker best show respect for, and acknowledge, your presence in the audience? Would you be most likely to be moved, influenced, shaped by a speaker who is adept at this effort?

This effort might involve some physical resources, such as eye contact, an attentive set of movements and gestures, and a varied use of vocal qualities; we explore these nonverbal resources in the section on delivery (see Chapter 18). In this chapter, we focus on how verbal resources can also help us respect and acknowledge our audience members. Consider again the observation Morrison (1994) made—quoted in Chapter 1—that "oppressive language does more than represent violence; it is violence; does more than represent the limits of knowledge; it limits knowledge" (p. 16). This suggests that language has power, which can manifest in public speaking in specific negative ways: committing violence, through demeaning listeners or trivializing their experiences and values, and limiting knowledge, through excluding listeners or denying them their own access to the material in your speech. Thus, conversely, using language effectively as a public speaker requires at least four practices that pursue goals directly opposite to these harmful outcomes—goals that treat audience members compassionately and inclusively rather than in violent or limiting ways:

1. Language should honor audience members' values.

2. Language should acknowledge particular audience members whenever possible.

3. Language should center on issues and examples relevant to audience members.

4. Language should encourage audience members to engage the material themselves.

This fourth goal, encouraging audience members to engage material themselves rather than simply "taking the speaker's word" for important ideas, can be most effectively accomplished through strong integration of *evidence* and careful use of *reasoning*, and we explore these efforts in depth in the following two chapters. Here, we will explore the first three goals as they relate to language and its role in public speaking.

Next, please read the text of President Barack Obama's speech delivered at an interfaith prayer vigil on December 16, 2012, in Newtown, Connecticut—2 days after the fatal shooting incident at Sandy Hook Elementary School in that community. You can find the full text of the speech on the U.S. White House website (http://www.whitehouse.gov/the-press-office/2012/12/16/remarks-president-sandy-hook-interfaith-prayer-vigil).

Please refer to this text in completing the following exercises.

Exercise 12A

1. *Language should honor audience members' values.* Now that you have read the text, what specific values do you believe would have been most important to the audience members at this event? Were those in attendance likely part of, or connected to, the families of the victims or families of emergency first responders? Given their relationship to the fatal shooting incident and the fact that it had taken place only 2 days earlier, what emotions would have been most prevalent for audience members? What themes would audience members have likely expected President Obama to highlight most strongly? Once you have considered these questions, list five specific words or phrases in this speech that reflect an attention to language that honors the values of audience members and that, thereby, helped President Obama speak with greater power.

    _____

    _____

    _____

    _____

    _____

2. *Language should acknowledge particular audience members.* Given how you imagined the audience in the previous exercise, consider who was present in the audience and whom President Obama had the opportunity to acknowledge, either directly or indirectly, in ways that gave his speech greater power. Direct acknowledgement usually involves naming a person or that person's title or profession, while indirect acknowledgment might involve making reference to an issue or concern distinctly associated with a specific group of audience members. Once you have considered again the identities of audience members, list five specific groups of people whom President Obama acknowledged (Hint: You will have to consider indirect acknowledgment to complete this list).

    _____

    _____

    _____

    _____

    _____

3. *Language should center on relevant issues and examples.* One way to recognize a significant social issue is that various people strongly affected by the issue will not necessarily agree on how to approach or resolve it. In the wake of the Sandy Hook shooting incident, there were disagreements on how best to make sense of the tragic loss of life, especially given that young people and educators who worked with young people were involved. How did President Obama craft a speech that could meaningfully foreground controversial issues and examples without alienating those in the audience who might disagree

about how best to make sense of this incident? Once you have considered these questions, list five specific words or phrases with which President Obama foregrounded issues or examples of great relevance to, and therefore having great power to shape the responses of, audience members.

_____

_____

_____

_____

_____

References

Morrison, T. (1994). *The Nobel lecture in literature, 1993*. New York: Knopf.

Obama, B. (2012, December 16). *Remarks by the President at Sandy Hook Interfaith Prayer Vigil*. Retrieved from http://www.whitehouse.gov/the-press-office/2012/12/16/remarks-president-sandy-hook-interfaith-prayer-vigil

CHAPTER 13

Evidence: Support for Your Main Ideas

Any speech you offer in a public context is, quite simply, only as compelling as the *evidence* you provide in support of your claims. This is as true for experienced speakers in public positions as it is for students in an introductory public speaking course. But evidence becomes especially important for novice speakers because it is one of the best ways to establish and maintain credibility with an audience (see Chapter 5). You can give yourself an effective speaking foundation by offering a variety of *types of evidence* and ensuring that you rely on the highest *quality of evidence*.

Types of Evidence

We characterize evidence as reflecting four basic types, based on both the initial source of the evidence and the purposes to which scholars and professionals usually put the evidence.

Statistical or Factual Evidence

This type of evidence consists of statistics, scientific findings, or other objective facts reported by credible experts. It is perhaps the type of evidence to which we most commonly ascribe "truth" value in American professional contexts, because we have been strongly influenced by post-Enlightenment, rational ideals suggesting that anything that can be objectively established is reliable and useful in the steady, progressive effort to fully understand our world. We have derived some important benefits and comforts from pursuing these ideals, from antibiotics and antiseptics to indoor plumbing to the computer on which we write these words. Our culture's idealization of these forms of evidence means that audience members will often find them highly compelling; so they can be quite useful for supporting your ideas and maintaining credibility.

However, this idealization can lead to the often inappropriate devaluing of the other types of evidence described here. Another drawback is that the procedures by which statistical or factual evidence is established are often highly technical and, therefore, open to careful examination only by experts whose work we come to trust by virtue of their training—meaning that speakers and audience members may be "skipping a step" in their evaluation of the quality of such evidence (more on this in the "Quality of Evidence" section). Finally, statistical evidence in particular can easily be used in misleading ways and lead to fallacious reasoning, because statistical evidence falls into two categories: descriptive and analytic. Descriptive statistics can isolate and quantify certain variables within the complex world in which we live, while analytic statistics can show the strength of relationships among these variables, indicating how much or how often the variables affect one another. Descriptive statistics cannot demonstrate causes, and even analytic statistics can indicate causation only within a carefully delineated set of relationships. Fallacies often result from interpreting close statistical relationships between two or more variables as "cause and effect" or "from the same cause," when in fact such causes may be only guesses.

Testimonial Evidence

This type of evidence consists of the exact, documented words of a person whose experience or perspective in some way directly addresses a specific idea (such as one of your supporting ideas). We commonly associate "testimony" with something offered by witnesses under oath in legal proceedings; however, people give testimony in other contexts as well, usually with the intention of confirming or disconfirming a specific idea, belief, or position. Some testimony accrues *prestige* because it is associated with a person whose words are given special weight; an obvious example is a medical doctor giving a formal opinion, but you are probably also familiar with corporations that use the testimonies of famous people to help sell their products. Other testimony may be offered by a *lay*person whose words do not usually have special weight but whose testimony has special value because of her or his perspective on events. Survivors of domestic violence, for example, may offer such testimony.

Anecdotal Evidence or Evidence From Example

This type of evidence consists of specific cases that can be documented, perhaps by the words of people involved or by secondary sources, and that have relevance to a given issue or idea. The educational profiles of students seeking public, postsecondary education, for instance—which might include reports of course titles, grade point averages, standardized test scores, and other qualifications—could each serve as an example within a speech about state support for public higher education. Examples are valuable because they can be juxtaposed with one another, giving audience members the sense of accumulated weight (*another* person who has a story like that?) and helping show commonalities that might support claims about underlying causes or useful solutions to problems. They are called "anecdotal," however, to distinguish them from carefully tested cases that are well defined and experimentally controlled in the search for "objective" evidence. An anecdotal example does not, in and of itself, preclude any number of counterexamples that may not have been identified yet; so public speakers must use care when offering this type of evidence, acknowledging that causal relationships or other commonalities are probable and not necessarily certain.

Descriptive or Narrative Evidence

This type of evidence often involves storytelling on the part of the public speaker, in which the speaker selects and shares experiences that are carefully stitched together into a compelling narrative. The power of this type of evidence is that it appeals to common sense, deriving its truthfulness value from the expectation that the narrative will "ring true" for most audience members, capturing aspects of our world that reflect "how things tend to go." Consider, for instance, how you know when a young child who is not yet an experienced storyteller is fibbing about a small detail; you likely recognize the fib because the child's narrative is not a good fit for the details described. This type of evidence is quite often questioned within the logic of rational, objective truth (see the "Statistical or Factual Evidence" section above), so speakers must use it carefully. However, it can be of great use in establishing and maintaining common ground with audience members, because they can feel empowered to judge its merits for themselves, rather than relying on technical expertise or on the word of others not present during the speech.

Notice that conceptualizing this type of evidence as "descriptive" also highlights the ways these evidence types can blend with one another and, therefore, require careful attention by public speakers to language and delivery. Imagine, for instance, a photograph of the shoreline on the coast of the Gulf of Mexico several months after the British Petroleum oil spill in April 2010. A speaker might consider that photo factual evidence and supplement it with scientific data or with the testimonies of those who live in the area, but the speaker will also, necessarily, select specific details within the photograph to highlight in a specific order. In this way, the speaker is integrating her or his own descriptive evidence with these other two forms of evidence.

The types of evidence you develop in conducting research to support your speech should be guided by two principles:

1. *Is this evidence appropriately compelling given the ideas of my speech?* This is why you should generate at least a tentative draft of your presentational outline, because if you have an initial sense of which specific ideas your speech will include, you can use this to spark your search for evidence.

2. *Is this evidence distinctly different in kind from other evidence I will offer my audience?* You can speak most credibly when you vary the types of evidence you offer, because this will encourage your audience to find the overall scope of your evidence more comprehensive and compelling (compared with using only a single type of evidence repeatedly) and because it will help maintain a lively quality to your speech and sustain audience members' interest and attention.

Exercise 13A

1. First, review your presentational outline for this speech (see Chapter 8). Notice that the outline exercises in that unit feature several *supporting ideas* that help develop each *main idea* in depth, and that each *supporting idea* might include two pieces of *evidence* that help establish that idea.

2. Next, use the worksheet below to list your *supporting ideas* and, under each *evidence* slot, identify one of the types of evidence described here that you think might best lend itself to helping establish that particular *supporting idea*. At this stage, you are only speculating so you have a starting point for your research; you might identify a different type of evidence than what you anticipate now.
   Use this key so you are writing only a single letter in each *evidence* slot:

   S: Statistical or factual evidence
   T: Testimony
   E: Anecdotal evidence or evidence from example
   D: Descriptive or narrative evidence

   Supporting idea: _____
   Evidence Type 1: _____   Evidence Type 2: _____

   Supporting idea: _____
   Evidence Type 1: _____   Evidence Type 2: _____

   Supporting idea: _____
   Evidence Type 1: _____   Evidence Type 2: _____

   Supporting idea: _____
   Evidence Type 1: _____   Evidence Type 2: _____

Supporting idea: _____
Evidence Type 1: _____   Evidence Type 2: _____

Supporting idea: _____
Evidence Type 1: _____   Evidence Type 2: _____

Supporting idea: _____
Evidence Type 1: _____   Evidence Type 2: _____

Supporting idea: _____
Evidence Type 1: _____   Evidence Type 2: _____

Supporting idea: _____
Evidence Type 1: _____   Evidence Type 2: _____

3. Next, review the worksheet. Do you see a variety of letters among the 18 evidence slots listed here? What evidence types dominate the list? What are your (compelling) reasons for using these types of evidence, given your speech topic?

_____

_____

_____

_____

_____

_____

_____

4. What evidence types do not appear anywhere on the list that you would like to make a special effort to identify in your research to enhance the variety of evidence you offer? What could you include, and why?

_____

_____

_____

_____

_____

_____

_____

Quality of Evidence

As the discussion of *types of evidence* above implied, not all evidence carries equal weight in all speaking situations. But all your evidence should be clearly marked for your audience as being of the highest *quality* currently available for that specific piece of evidence. Suppose, for example, that you are accumulating statistical evidence to support your speech regarding the urgent need for increased state support for public higher education. You are thrilled to have found a study claiming that over a 5-year period, graduates from public colleges and universities earned 5% more in annual overall income than graduates from private colleges and universities. But not so fast; consider, first, what makes a series of statistical claims of high quality. Three considerations would apply here:

1. Is the information as *current* as possible?

2. Is the information appropriate in *scope* (i.e., is it as relevant as possible)?

3. Is the information published by a *reputable* source?

Taking these one by one, using our example, will help us explore how these three considerations can guide your effort to use high-quality evidence.

1. Is the information as *current* as possible?

This consideration is especially significant for statistical and factual evidence, because this type of evidence derives its power from its relationship to the steady accumulation of knowledge. Even carefully established objective "facts" are often modified or even discarded as, over time, new knowledge emerges and new relationships among facts are discovered. If the "5-year period" of your income-level study is 15 years prior to your speech, the state economy, or the nature of colleges and universities, might have changed enough over time to make those claims invalid. For each piece of evidence you offer, you should ensure that no subsequent information has superseded or challenged it. This means striving to use the most current scholarly sources available in your school's library.

2. Is the information appropriate in *scope* (i.e., is it as relevant as possible)?

This consideration is especially significant for testimonial or anecdotal evidence, because these types of evidence depend on human communication—and people do not know, when they offer their testimonies or stories, what use might be made of their communication at a later time. In our example, careful examination might reveal that the study was conducted only among college and university graduates who took jobs within the same state from which they graduated. Does your conclusion change if you consider this information? How might the study be skewed by the exclusion of graduates employed out of state? For each piece of evidence you offer, you should ensure that you have considered the initial purpose and/or intent for which the evidence was generated, as much as you can determine from the evidence itself. Avoid citing statistics that you have isolated from much more complex studies, avoid using direct quotes that shift the intended meaning by taking the author's words out of their original context, and avoid omitting details associated with the piece of evidence because you fear that those details will weaken the power of the evidence.

3. Is the information published by a *reputable* source?

This consideration is highly significant for any piece of evidence you offer. Always begin your search for relevant evidence by consulting scholarly sources, usually those found in your school's library of academic research (digital or physical). If you identify evidence that has not been published by a scholarly source, seriously consider the perspective of the publisher: Perhaps if your study about graduate income levels had not been published by a scholarly journal but instead by a government agency, that evidence would be slightly less reliable, but not much. If that same study had been both conducted and published by a nonprofit think tank established for the purpose of promoting public higher education, it would be a bit less reliable, though still relevant as long as you carefully acknowledged the source. If that same study had been published by a prominent web blogger, it would again be somewhat less credible. If the same study were one you initially found on a friend's personal webpage, it would lack the credibility necessary to enhance your speech and you should discard it. Notice that this train of potential publication sources could give you a trail to follow and thus bolster the credibility of the evidence: If your friend had published it but provided a link to the prominent blogger whose site she found it on, and then when you checked the blogger's site you found a citation for the think tank's webpage, you would have a source you could, conceivably, introduce in your speech. Were you to do so, you would want to cite only the most credible source to which you could reliably and accurately trace the publication of the evidence; in other words, as long as the think tank's site had actually published the study (and if it was appropriate in scope and current), you should cite only that website, not the other steps "lower" on the credibility trail.

CHAPTER 14

Reasoning

How you combine evidence and reasoning to encourage audience members to share your conclusions is the core of an effective public speech. One way we can illustrate why reasoning is important for a public speaker is to explore a brief moment of dialogue that occurred as we were writing at Deanna's home, which has three doors leading to the outside: Deanna was asked by someone in the house to close the "back door," and Keith offered to do it instead. But in watching Deanna close the "back door" more quickly than she could accept his offer, Keith realized that he would have actually closed a different door—one leading to the garage, rather than the sliding-glass door to the patio that Deanna closed and that, evidently, is called the "back door" in Deanna's family. Notice that when we speak face to face, different understandings of what is true can often be usefully untangled through clarification, because in such settings speakers and listeners can interact immediately and flexibly. But in a public speaking setting, responsive turn-taking and conversational branching are often ruled out, or postponed, by formal speaking contexts. So getting "on the same page" with your audience, as a public speaker, is vital. Yet shared reasoning and shared conclusions are often challenging to achieve and require great care.

For instance, the brief difference in understanding between Deanna and Keith about which door is properly the "back door" might seem to be a matter of simple semantics: One person commonly uses the label "back door" to refer to a specific door in her own home, while another, unfamiliar with this bit of family communication, misunderstands how the label is applied. But the choice in any home to call one particular door the "back door" rests on the surface, often taken for granted, of more deeply rooted cognitive processes that organize ideas and relationships among ideas. We call these cognitive processes "reasoning," and though we engage in taken-for-granted reasoning, drawing conclusions constantly in our everyday lives, when we speak in public we need to carefully examine our reasoning if we hope to draw conclusions that make sense to our audience.

To show how reasoning affects our everyday life, let's consider what underlies the designation "back door": Any house with a back door must, by implication, have more than one outside door—and if you understand that, you are using reasoning to do so, even if it takes only a quick "recognition" that doesn't feel much like "reasoning" in the moment. In a house with exactly two doors leading to the outside, can there be only a "front door" and a "back door," with no other possibilities? Could a house have only a "front door" and a "side door," or a "front door" and a "kitchen door"? Would these labels make sense to you, given your experience? Would it make a difference if the place was an apartment rather than a house? Would it make a difference if, in a house with two outside doors, one led to the garage, so that the doors were called the "front door" and the "garage door"?

We can explore, using these questions, how different forms of reasoning might lead us to different possible answers. Three different forms of reasoning we will explore are deductive, inductive, and analogical reasoning.

Exercise 14A

1. To practice recognizing this process of reasoning, watch again the compelling YouTube clip you chose for the exercises in Chapter 11, on compassionate criticism.

Deductive Reasoning

One common way we reason—and perhaps the way we most often tend to think of "reasoning" as an academic concept—is called *deductive reasoning*. This involves beginning with an initial premise and then using that premise to come to conclusions about specific cases. If you believe that a house with only one outside door cannot ever meaningfully have a "back door," you are using deductive reasoning, like this:

1. Naming a specific type of door, rather than just saying "the door," is meaningful only when a dwelling has more than one outside door.

2. This house has only one outside door.

3. Therefore, it is meaningless to call that one door the "back door."

Notice that when using deductive reasoning, you are moving toward a *certainty*—toward a conclusion that must follow, without exception, from your general principles. The scientific method you might have learned when doing experiments in science labs or mathematical proofs you might have learned in geometry or algebra courses are examples of deductive reasoning that leads to conclusions that are certain. Also, notice that there are two primary ways we might use deductive reasoning weakly: Either our initial premise might be false (maybe we *can* meaningfully name different types of doors even in houses with just one outside door), or our attempt to apply the principle to one specific case might be a mistake (this house is not a typical case for some reason, maybe because it is a duplex with residences split front to back, so the principle doesn't properly apply). We will return to these two possible weak uses of deductive reasoning later in this chapter.

Exercise 14B

1. Identify an example of deductive reasoning used in your chosen YouTube clip. The conclusion the clip urges us to accept might be implied rather than explicitly stated.

_____

_____

_____

_____

_____

_____

_____

Inductive Reasoning

A form of reasoning we use often in everyday life, as shown by the "back door" series of questions, is *inductive reasoning*. We don't likely have any doubts about back doors in a house with just one door, but in the example above, when there are three outside doors, we are usually relying on accumulated past experience of similar cases to draw conclusions. We have likely been in other homes with multiple outside doors, and we reason about which door might be called the "back door" in a new environment by recalling those experiences and deciding which door is most likely to have this label. Notice that when using inductive reasoning, we are reaching conclusions that are *probable* rather than certain, by reasoning from multiple other specific cases that are like this new case. This makes the temptation to overgeneralize a significant risk when we use inductive reasoning to build a case in favor of a single conclusion. Also, notice that we can use inductive reasoning weakly in one other way, shared with deductive reasoning: The specific case in question might not match the supposedly "similar" previous cases in some important way. We will return to these two possible weak uses of inductive reasoning later in this chapter.

Exercise 14C

1. Identify an example of inductive reasoning used in your chosen YouTube clip. The conclusion the clip urges us to accept might be implied rather than explicitly stated.

Analogical Reasoning

Another form of reasoning that becomes important in everyday life, even when we don't necessarily recognize we are using it, is *analogical reasoning*, which means drawing conclusions based on analogies. An analogy involves comparing one idea you believe your audience knows well to another idea that may be new or uncertain for them. A statement like, "A state educating its citizens is like a whole family helping raise its children," would be an analogy. The more effective the comparison, the more likely your audience members will accept the conclusion. An analogy is different from a metaphor or simile, however, such as the claim, "My love is like a red, red rose" by Scottish poet Robert Burns. In a metaphor or simile, we choose the familiar idea in the comparison ("a red, red rose") because it has simple, core, intense qualities that audience members can quickly recognize as they strive to better understand the unfamiliar idea ("my love"). In an analogy, the familiar and unfamiliar ideas are both usually more complex and nuanced, such as raising children and educating citizens.

Suppose, following our example, that you are looking at a split-level house built into a hillside. The street level of the house contains a garage with a walkway off to the left side, up a short, steep slope that leads into the house through an undecorated, hardly visible door. An elegant series of steps with a bannister curls gradually upward, around the right side of the garage to a level above, where there is a fancy door with an archway and a doorbell; this door faces away from the street. If you were a guest invited to this house, wouldn't you climb the steps and ring the doorbell above the garage? And if you did so and were invited into the house, and heard someone in the family refer to the "back door," would you reasonably assume that she or he meant the door below, near the garage, even though it's actually the only outside door facing the street? Reasoning this way would be reasoning from analogy. Though this home might be quite different from any other home you've encountered, you focus on the fact that it shares many features in common with other homes, features especially significant to the "back door" question: It has multiple outside doors; it has one prominent, decorated and one less prominent, undecorated door, and guests use one door rather than the other. You use these features to draw a probable conclusion, but this form of reasoning is different from inductive reasoning because it is not based on a series of closely related, common cases. However, the two risks inherent in analogical reasoning are the same as the risks when we use inductive reasoning: We might overgeneralize when arguing for a single conclusion, or we might assume common links that are not really relevant.

Exercise 14D

1. Identify an example of analogical reasoning used in your chosen YouTube clip. The conclusion the clip urges us to accept might be implied rather than explicitly stated.

_____

_____

_____

_____

_____

_____

_____

The Effective Integration of Claims and Evidence: Avoiding Weak or Fallacious Reasoning

As we noted above, when we speak in public, we must attend more directly to our reasoning—to why our conclusions are appropriate—than we typically do in everyday life. As we will demonstrate below, attending carefully to reasoning, both when preparing and when delivering your speech, flows from a conception of public speaking as dialogic, because when we do so, we ensure that our claims make us *more* worthy of our listeners' attention and demonstrate *more* respect for their perspectives. Attending carefully to reasoning involves three steps as a public speaker:

1. Building a strong foundation of evidence for your speech

2. Explicitly examining your reasoning when developing your speech, including checking for weak or fallacious reasoning

3. Using language in your speech that highlights the path an audience can take toward accepting your conclusions, by clarifying your reasoning

In the previous chapter, we explored building a foundation of evidence as support for your main ideas. We turn now to how you can examine your reasoning as you prepare your speech and how you can include language in your speech that highlights your conviction in your reasoning.

Clarifying Reasoning and Avoiding Fallacies

The way to build an effective relationship between reasoning and evidence is to distinguish between the *evidence* in your speech and the *claims* you make about that evidence. One way to understand reasoning is to realize that it is the thread that stitches together your claims and your evidence. We often take reasoning for granted in everyday situations because we assume that the immediate, shared evidence available is enough to persuade one another of our claims—we expect others to make quick leaps directly from evidence to claims. If you and I are both looking from the street at the split-level house described above and I say, pointing to the undecorated downstairs door, "Hah! That's the 'back door' even though it's the only one facing the street," I'm assuming that the evidence is grounded in our shared experience. If you disagree with my claim that it's the "back door," you might ask for more evidence before you agree, or you might ask me to clarify my reasoning.

However, public speaking contexts require speakers to anticipate disagreements about speech claims before those disagreements happen—bolstering your claims in advance with good evidence, as we discussed in the previous chapter, and encouraging your audience members to accept your claims because they recognize the strength in your reasoning as you speak. You can highlight your reasoning and demonstrate its value for audience members by using language appropriate to the form of reasoning you have chosen.

Deductive Reasoning

If you are using deductive reasoning to link your evidence to claims, a structure such as this one can highlight the power of your reasoning:

Given that [insert a basic principle or already demonstrated idea that your audience accepts], then when we see [insert a phrase summarizing a piece of evidence], we must conclude [insert a primary claim you want to make].

You can and should vary your deductive reasoning–based language, but you can rely on this structure because it epitomizes the power of conclusions based on deductive, certain reasoning. You might make substitutions such as these:

- *Because, since, as we know,* in place of *given*
- *Notice, consider, recognize,* in place of *see*
- *Accept, choose, realize,* in place of *conclude*

Inductive Reasoning

If you are using inductive reasoning to link your evidence to claims, a structure such as this one can highlight the power of your reasoning:

Cases such as these [insert a series of phrases summarizing several pieces of evidence] indicate [insert a primary claim you want to make].

You can and should vary your inductive reasoning–based language, but you can rely on this structure because it epitomizes the power of conclusions based on inductive, probabilistic reasoning. You might make substitutions such as these:

- *Examples, experiences, situations,* in place of *cases*
- *Suggest, make likely, predict,* in place of *indicate*

Analogical Reasoning

If you are using analogical reasoning to link your evidence to claims, a structure such as this one can highlight the power of your reasoning:

[Insert a primary claim you want to make] is like [insert a description of an idea that your audience already accepts].

You can and should vary your analogical reasoning–based language, but you can rely on this structure because it epitomizes the power of conclusions based on analogical, comparative reasoning. You might make substitutions such as these:

- *Parallels, is similar to, is comparable to,* in place of *is like*

Avoiding Fallacies

Fallacious reasoning results from advancing claims that are not well supported by your evidence or are weak uses of one of the three types of reasoning discussed in this chapter. As we have discussed, you can refer to Chapter 13 for help developing evidence that supports your claims well. Here, we discuss how to avoid weak uses of reasoning.

The most common way to develop a fallacy, rather than a strong claim, when using *deductive reasoning* is to choose a piece of evidence that is a poor fit for the initial premise. Another fallacious use of deductive reasoning is to begin with a false, or poorly stated, initial premise. Either of these can result in a fallacy called a *non sequitur*, meaning a conclusion that "does not follow." Consider these two examples and try to spot the weak reasoning in each that results in a non sequitur fallacy:

- Given that our state guarantees a spot at a public college or university for all high school graduates with a 2.0 high school GPA or better, and given that Robin never received any high school grade below a B, the state should guarantee Robin a spot at a public college or university.

- Given that our state funds public colleges and universities to fulfill the mission of educating all qualified high school graduates in this state, and given that Robin is a qualified high school graduate in this state, the state should guarantee Robin a spot at a public college or university.

You can avoid fallacies of deductive reasoning by carefully stating your initial premise and your specific case, showing your audience that the case is a perfect fit for the initial premise and that, therefore, they must accept your conclusion.

The most common way to develop a fallacy, rather than a strong claim, when using *inductive reasoning* is to overgeneralize from the specific cases you articulate, called a *hasty generalization* fallacy. This results from reaching for a conclusion more broad-based than the specific cases compel. Another common way to develop a fallacy when using this type of reasoning, because inductive conclusions often offer summary statements that link together various specific cases, is the *moralistic* fallacy, in which a series of *facts* about specific cases are used to offer a conclusion that is not factual but, instead, is based in *values*. A third common way to develop an inductive reasoning–based fallacy is the *slippery slope* fallacy, in which past outcomes are offered to support a conclusion about a similar but more widespread future outcome that in fact cannot be predicted. Consider these three examples and try to spot the weak reasoning in each that results from either a hasty generalization, a moralistic fallacy, or a slippery slope fallacy:

■ Because earning a bachelor's degree will net a typical person hundreds of thousands of dollars in additional income, compared with someone who has earned only a high school diploma (Adams, 2011, para. 9), and because the 20 high school graduates introduced in this speech have met all the qualifications to be admitted to a public college or university, yet have not been admitted this year, the state is cheating those graduates if it does not offer them spots in these colleges or universities.

■ Because earning a bachelor's degree will net a typical person hundreds of thousands of dollars in additional income in comparison with someone who has earned only a high school diploma, and because the 20 high school graduates introduced in this speech have met all the qualifications to be admitted to a public college or university, yet have not been admitted this year, the state will continue to suffer financially if it does not more fully and reliably invest in public education.

■ Because earning a bachelor's degree will net a typical person hundreds of thousands of dollars in additional income in comparison with someone who has earned only a high school diploma, and because the 20 high school graduates introduced in this speech have met all the qualifications to be admitted to a public college or university, yet have not been admitted this year, the state has inadequate procedures for ensuring that qualified applicants have spots waiting for them at public colleges or universities.

You can avoid fallacies of inductive reasoning by examining your conclusion statement and considering whether what it predicts is the *only* likely outcome that will follow from the conditions in your specific series of cases (this will prevent the hasty generalization and slippery slope fallacies), and by maintaining a clear distinction in language between facts and values (this will prevent the moralistic fallacy).

The two common ways to develop fallacies, rather than strong claims, when using *analogical reasoning* are to offer a *false analogy* that reflects a poor fit between the two compared examples and to imply a single, common cause that accounts for outcomes across the two compared examples (called the *fallacy of the single cause*). Consider these two examples and try to spot the weak analogical reasoning in each that results from either a false analogy or a fallacy of the single cause:

■ A state educating its citizenry is like a family caring for its young; so the allocation of resources toward postsecondary education should be the primary purpose of a state's budget.

■ A state educating its citizenry is like a family caring for its young; so the only good reason for abandoning state funding after secondary school would be an embrace of the perception that postsecondary students are old enough to provide for themselves without additional support.

You can avoid fallacies of analogical reasoning not only by choosing analogies that are familiar to and resonant with your audience members but also by relying only on analogies that reflect a complex, multi-part fit among their various elements, ensuring that relationships among all (or most) parts of complex systems are parallel across the two compared examples. Note that the fallacy of the single cause is a pitfall often associated not only with comparative examples such as analogies but also with statistically documented patterns of outcomes, because statistical data are often descriptive, not analytic (see Chapter 13); so speakers sometimes mistakenly attribute causes to statistical data not designed to track causes.

Reference

Adams, C. (2011, May 11). Study chronicles financial benefits of bachelor's degree. *Education Week.* Retrieved from http://blogs.edweek.org/edweek/college_bound/2011/05/study_chronicles_financial_benefits_of_a_bachelors_degree.html

CHAPTER 15
Conclusions

Conclusions, like leave-taking rituals where you review next steps or wish someone well, help create meaningful and sometimes lasting relationships, and that is true in the public speaking context as well. What you share with your audience at the end of your speech is at least as important as what you share with them at the outset; while you can make the most of what researchers call primacy effect in your introduction, your conclusion—and what researchers refer to as recency effect—can help you leave a lasting impression. You can make the most of the primacy effect when you remember and plan for the ways your listeners will make important decisions about your ideas based on the first things you say to them. In contrast, an awareness of the recency effect, of how audience members will remember and take action on ideas and impressions they develop from the last things they hear you discuss, will help you develop a strong, compelling conclusion. A well-crafted conclusion reviews the main ideas of your speech, implicates listeners in the goal(s) of your speech and provides them with next steps to pursue, and leaves listeners to reflect on a powerful and memorable closing idea or statement. We'll address each of these three components here.

1. *A well-crafted conclusion reviews the main ideas of your speech.* If an important outcome of an introduction is to create a sense of anticipation, then an equally important outcome for the conclusion is to create a sense of closure. Closure in a speech, just like closure in our relationships or other aspects of our lives, helps provide us with a sense of completion, and perhaps satisfaction or renewed purpose. To signal to your listeners that you are nearing the end of your speech, you can review with them what you have explored during your time together. We might casually refer to this as a review statement or review, and it is the inverse of the preview speakers share in the introduction. Returning to our speech asking listeners to urge California's Governor Brown to reestablish adequate funding to public colleges and universities, here's an example of a review statement:

> Let's review what we've discussed here: First, we addressed the benefits of a college education and why affordable access is so important, especially for first-generation college students. Second, we reviewed Governor Brown's higher-education appropriation decisions and how they have affected who has been able to attend college. Finally, we explored how restoring the state budget to 2009–2010 apportion levels would make it so students like Robin—students like many of us here—are better able to take advantage of the opportunities higher education affords.

2. *A well-crafted conclusion implicates listeners in the goal(s) of your speech and provides them with next steps to pursue.* To achieve your purpose as a speaker, whether that purpose is to teach your listeners something new or convince them to take action on a particular issue, it is important to remind them not only of your intentions as a speaker but also of how they are implicated in—how they influence and are influenced

by—the issues you address in your speech. In restating your thesis, you remind your listeners of the purpose of your speech and what you expect of them in return for listening. Further, while it is generally a poor idea to introduce new material in a conclusion, it is important to remind your listeners of the next steps you believe they should take (e.g., how they can use that new information or where they can participate in a local protest). This functions as a kind of rallying cry that helps listeners take purpose and meaning from your time together.

For instance, as you'll recall, this was our thesis statement from that same example speech:

Public colleges and universities like ours provide necessary access to higher education for students like Robin here in California, but recent funding trends limit this access. We should each write to Governor Brown and urge him to restore the state budget to the apportion levels of 2009–2010 so all qualified candidates will have the access we enjoy.

As part of the conclusion, we might restate this thesis as follows:

Therefore, it is absolutely essential that each of us writes to Governor Brown, urging him to restore our state budget to these earlier levels.

Then you can continue the conclusion by identifying next steps the listeners can take:

Here is a template you can use to develop your own letter to the governor. I've left spaces where you can describe the ways affordable higher education has been or will be critical to your own success.

3. *A well-crafted conclusion leaves listeners to reflect on a powerful and memorable closing statement or idea.* Knowing that your listeners will more likely retain information from the first and final ideas you share in your speech can help you strengthen both your introduction and conclusion. The first idea(s) you share in your speech occur in your attention-getter, where you draw listeners in to your topic/argument; the final idea(s) you share in your speech occur in your conclusion and, more precisely, what we often casually refer to as a "clincher." The strongest clincher speaks back to or echoes the opening attention-getter in a memorable and well-crafted way.

Here's how our sample introduction opened:

I think most of us are pretty thankful for this opportunity to be in college, right? Even when we're tired and beat up at finals, we know that getting a college degree will make a difference in our own and our families' lives. Robin, for instance, whose family is working class going back many generations, has worked hard to achieve qualifying grades for college but has not earned the grades or standardized test scores that a private university would respond to with a large scholarship award. Robin needs to earn more money than just enough to live as a student because the family needs additional financial support; so any school Robin chooses must be within close driving distance of home. How can Robin earn an accredited degree without access to a local, affordable state college? According to a study by the American Institutes for Research and Nexus Research and Policy Center, earning that bachelor's degree will net you between 300,000 and 550,000 in additional income in comparison with someone who has earned only a high school diploma (Adams, 2011, para. 9). That's a lot of money—and just imagine what you can do if you save or invest it! But as taxpayers and state governments reduce funding for public colleges and universities, fewer people will have access to the opportunities we now enjoy.

Echoing back key themes from this attention-getting material will help create a sense of closure for your listeners, inviting them to reflect on your argument in lasting and meaningful ways. A clincher for this speech might pick up that connection to the listeners—how thankful they are for the opportunity to attend college—revisit the hypothetical example of Robin, and remind listeners of the stakes involved in this issue. For example:

> If we all write Governor Brown, we can help him understand what affordable access to college means to us. And in the time it would take for us to vent to our friends about juggling all our responsibilities during finals, we could make a difference in our own lives and the lives of all the Robins in our state. As you'll recall, each one of us who successfully completes college will earn between 300,000 and 550,000 in additional income; all of us together—and the additional income we generate—can help California and its citizens thrive for generations to come.

Exercise 15A

Now it's your turn. Try to develop your conclusion for an upcoming presentation here, taking care to address each of these three components.

1. Review the two to five main ideas that supported your thesis.

_____

_____

_____

_____

_____

_____

_____

2. Restate your thesis, and cue your audience members to their next steps.

_____

_____

_____

_____

_____

_____

_____

3. Create a lasting and memorable impression by revisiting your attention-getting material.

_____

_____

_____

_____

_____

_____

_____

Remember that you can find additional guidance on drafting conclusions in SpeechPlanner (speechplanner.sagepub.com).

CHAPTER 16

Presentational Aids

Presentational aids can be quite valuable in enhancing your ability to speak effectively in a public setting. Indeed, your public speaking instructor might require that you use them so you can practice working with them and better grasp their value. Presentational aids can

1. enhance your credibility;
2. stimulate the attention of audience members; and
3. clarify complex ideas, relationships, and pieces of evidence.

Most important, however, presentational aids should always *complement* your speech; they should never *stand in* for any part of your speech or *replace* any part of your speech, and they should not be used in ways that draw audience members' attention away from you. As you will see in the list of questions at the end of this section, you should be able to give the same speech, with the same quality, even if all your presentational aids were suddenly unavailable to you.

Enhancing Credibility

Presentational aids enhance credibility by demonstrating your careful preparation for the public speaking opportunity. When you develop effective presentational aids, you show that you are attentive to the visual, auditory, and cognitive needs of audience members because you provide opportunities to help audience members better visualize your ideas, see and hear for themselves important pieces of supporting evidence, and receive necessary information in multiple modes that range beyond what you can do with your own voice and body. All these assets of presentational aids bolster your credibility not only because they show respect for the audience's needs as a partner in dialogue but also—even more important—because they grant audience members greater autonomy. An audience member whom you support by providing direct access to evidence or additional means to grasp your ideas can more consistently and independently judge the merits of your evidence and your reasoning.

Exercise 16A

1. Return now to the list of evidence you developed in Chapter 13. What two pieces of evidence would be better received if your audience members could see or hear something for themselves? The presentational form might be photographs or moving images; a series of words from a person's testimony or anecdote that, because they were carefully chosen, are especially important in terms of recognizing the

words themselves; words recorded as they were spoken, as in a song, film scene, public speech, podcast, or YouTube clip; or a statistical claim that can be demonstrated using a line or bar graph.

Evidence: _____
Form in which audience members can see/hear for themselves: _____

Evidence: _____
Form in which audience members can see/hear for themselves: _____

Stimulating the Attention of Audience Members

Presentational aids can also enhance your speech by helping create a more lively, engaging environment through which your audience members can appreciate your speech. Though the central focus of a public speech should always be on the speaker and not on the presentational aids, many audience members will find it easier to maintain attention throughout the entirety of your speech if they can, from time to time, look at and/or listen to something besides you. Recognizing this does not entail doubting yourself as a speaker; most people find it difficult to concentrate two senses, such as the eyes and ears, on a single focal point for a long period of time, without engaging their other senses or shifting their viewing and listening focus.

Exercise 16B

1. Return now to your presentational outline from Chapter 8. What two elements of this outline (these might be pieces of evidence or main or supporting ideas) might lend themselves to sights or sounds that keep audience members interested and/or give audience members something fresh to consider? If you choose evidence, these might be intrinsically interesting sights, such as still or moving images; pieces of evidence you could make visually interesting with a bit of effort, such as charts, graphs, lists, sequences, or chronologies to which you could add color or style; or intrinsically interesting sounds, such as a person's speaking voice or music. If you choose main or supporting ideas, how might they suggest a theme you can use to create related images, sounds, or other sensory experiences (e.g., smells, tastes, items to touch) that can transform the classroom experience?

    Evidence/theme: _____
    Presentational aid that stimulates audience members' senses: _____

    Evidence/theme: _____
    Presentational aid that stimulates audience members' senses: _____

Clarifying Complex Ideas

Perhaps the most important use of presentational aids is that they can help audience members grapple with ideas that are more difficult to grasp in an oral/aural context or, especially, in a one-to-many speaking context. You are likely familiar with aids that serve this purpose. They include enlarged graphs and charts showing how numbers relate to one another or how patterns change over time or place; slides that function as outlines of your speech, with title slides showing major parts of your speech and bullet points showing how smaller ideas relate to larger ones; and slides that increase the size or importance of key speech elements, such as visual evidence or special words and phrases.

Exercise 16C

1. Return now to your presentational outline from Chapter 8. What two elements of this outline (these might be pieces of evidence or main or supporting ideas) might need clarification or might audience members need to attend to carefully?

    Evidence/theme: _____

    Presentational aid that enhances clarity: _____

    Evidence/theme: _____

    Presentational aid that enhances clarity: _____

Creating and Using Presentational Aids Effectively

Once you have identified worthwhile opportunities to integrate presentational aids into your public speech, you must ensure that these enhance, rather than detract from, your speech. Ask this series of questions for each presentational aid you develop:

■ Do you need this presentational aid? Is your speech distinctly better with this aid than without it? If the answer is "no," discard it.

■ Can this presentational aid be integrated smoothly, on its own, into the speech? People often make extensive use of PowerPoint or Prezi for this purpose, ensuring that a mere click of a button can advance slides or focus on frames. But if you use other types of presentational aids, can each one be used when and how it is needed, even while you speak? Definitely *avoid* passing out items to the audience while you speak, as this detracts attention from you, the speaker.

■ If you use words (such as on a projected slide or frame, or on a poster), is each word legible to all audience members, regardless of where they are seated?

■ If you use slides or frames (such as PowerPoint or Prezi), do you provide only minimal information—just the most important—on each slide or frame? Avoid cluttering your slides or frames with too many words or pictures; generally, more than five lines of text or more than two images on any single slide/frame challenges or distracts audience members rather than enhancing clarity.

■ If you use slides or frames, do you use moving parts such as animations only once per element at the most, and generally no more than once or twice per slide/frame? Too many moving elements challenge or distract audience members rather than sharpening their attention.

■ If you use nondigital, physical presentational aids such as photographs or posters, can all audience members see all the elements on the aid, no matter where they are seated? Have you used letters, lines, and colors that are easy to read? Avoid using many different colors when developing charts or graphs because, again, these can challenge or distract audience members rather than enhancing clarity.

■ If you are using electronic aids such as computer-driven presentation programs or sounds, do you understand how to control them? Have you rehearsed with them in advance? Can you still deliver your speech effectively if the technology fails?

CHAPTER 17

Practice

We title this chapter "practice" rather than "rehearsal" for two important reasons, which we explore in this section. First, public speaking is an emergent communicative process responsive to the moment of the speech. Although public speeches often occur in formal contexts, they are less carefully marked than plays, monologues, and other aesthetic performances. *Rehearsal* connotes a gradual movement toward precise, repeatable, distinctively recognizable aesthetic choices, even when these choices might not be exactly the same in each performance. In contrast, *practice* connotes strengthening a skill, such as the muscle memory of an athlete or the sight reading of a musician. When you prepare to speak in public, you do not want your choices to be "repeatable" or "distinctively recognizable," because in almost all cases, you will deliver this speech only once or, if in a competition, perhaps a few times at most. You do, however, want each speaking opportunity to strengthen your skill as a speaker, enabling you to accomplish each goal you set for yourself with greater confidence and with a broader range of embodied skills (including voice, gesture, eye contact, muscle tension, and kinesthetic awareness of your audience and the environment) each time you speak. Practicing your speech in advance gives you the opportunity to build confidence and broaden your skills before you engage your audience so you can show your audience respect and enhance your credibility with them by offering your most effective speaking performance.

Exercise 17A

1. Explain, in your own words, how you can recognize a well-prepared speaker who respects her or his audience members and their time and attention. What specific choices does this speaker make that enable you to recognize effective preparation?

_____

_____

_____

_____

_____

_____

_____

2. How does this speaker's voice indicate preparation?

_____

_____

_____

_____

_____

_____

3. How does this speaker's use of eye contact and facial expression reflect preparation?

_____

_____

_____

_____

_____

_____

4. How does this speaker's body, apart from voice and face, reflect preparation?

_____

_____

_____

_____

_____

_____

The second reason we choose *practice* rather than *rehearsal* relates to our conception of public speaking as dialogue. Too often, we unreflectively treat public speaking as an "onstage" moment in which audience members await the speaker's arrival, having already signaled their interest in the upcoming message as concertgoers signal theirs by buying tickets and wearing the appropriate T-shirts. But as we have shown, most public communication is more complex and multifaceted than a one-time, one-directional opportunity on a fixed stage for an eager audience. The level of eagerness of your colleagues in class, for instance, can help complicate this notion right away. Moreover, a dialogic conception of public speaking reminds us that, in a relational frame, our speech stimulates fresh, unexpected responses from an audience with diverse needs and interests. We cannot meaningfully "rehearse" for this audience any more than we can "rehearse" for family conversations at a large holiday dinner table. We can, however, practice our dinner-table skills by sharpening our attentiveness, becoming more confident and self-aware when we use our communicative resources, and deepening our knowledge of and curiosity about ourselves, others, and the world. These same goals ground how we can best practice for a public speech.

Exercise 17B

1. Describe three of your strengths as a public speaker. You might recognize these strengths from previous speeches you have given or ways you have engaged people or ideas in your everyday life.

   _____

   _____

   _____

2. Describe three ways you look forward to improving as a public speaker. You might recognize these needed improvements from previous speeches you have given or ways you have engaged people or ideas in your everyday life.

   _____

   _____

   _____

So much for *why* you should practice—and you already know *who* should practice. An easy way to organize your practice efforts is to choose *what*, *when*, and *where* you will practice.

What

Choosing *what* you will practice might seem easy, but you can make your practice efforts most effective by beginning with this step. You should make careful choices about content and delivery in choosing what you will practice. "Chunking" your speech is a useful process for managing content during practice sessions. Focusing on growth is helpful for managing delivery choices during practice sessions.

Chunking

This method involves separating your material into segments that have coherent meaning in and of themselves, then committing to practice that treats each segment with equal importance. This has two advantages: First, it helps you learn your speech more effectively than starting at the beginning each time, which often leads to an excellent first half of the speech and a weak second half marked by forgetfulness and lower energy (you have probably witnessed speeches like this). Second, it makes the speech easier to manage, because small segments can be more easily learned than an entire speech as a whole.

One good starting point for chunking is your full-sentence outline, which should distinguish internally meaningful chunks of your speech's content, such as an introduction, main points with topic sentences, supporting evidence for each main point, transitions, and a conclusion. Let's say you are practicing a speech with four main points framed by an introduction and a conclusion. You might work just with each main point's topic sentences for the first two or three practice sessions, right after you create your outline. Get to know these claims well enough that you can anticipate how each claim seems to cry out for supporting evidence. Next, start bringing that support into the practice session; perhaps tackle one of the main points by itself for each of the next four practice sessions. You should find, after that fourth "main point with support" session, that you could comfortably explain to a friend or family member, without any notes, how each main point relates to its support. Then, forget about those main points for the next few sessions, and focus only on the introduction and conclusion. Make sure, however, that you organize your work and that you devote at least one entire session, late in the preparation process, to practicing transitions—nothing else. Ideally, this should be your last step before speaking. "Sew" the key sentences (last and first) of each main point together with your well-developed, logical transitions. If you devote an entire session just to practicing transitions, late in the process, you should find that this session helps reinforce your entire speech—functioning as a "whole speech" style practice session, even if it takes less time because you focus only on the transition moments themselves.

Exercise 17C

1. Identify at least seven distinct "segments" of your speech. Remember that these should be internally meaningful *groups* of ideas; so they need not be "seven distinct paragraphs" (remember that transitions, for example, would be a good segment to list here).
   Content Segments

   _____

   _____

   _____

   _____

   _____

   _____

   _____

   _____

   _____

Make sure to devote at least one practice session to *each* of these segments!

Focusing on Growth

A useful way to build confidence when practicing delivery elements is to focus on how you would like to *grow* as a speaker, in terms of how you use your voice, face, and body. This is important for two reasons:

First, it organizes the work during practice sessions; second, it focuses your anxiety in a productive, rather than destructive, way. To explain how an emphasis on growth helps organize the work, consider this example: One of the authors took high school biology classes from a teacher who, among many odd quirks, would stand in front of the class on every exam review day and say the same thing, over and over, at various points in the review: "Don't study what you *know*. Study what you *don't* know." This teacher's concern was similar to our chunking discussion: He wanted the students, if they were preparing for a 50-question exam, to use their precious study time on the 25 or 30 terms they did not already know, rather than trying to divide the material into 50 tiny, much less useful pieces devoted equally to each term on the study list.

Similarly, you can enhance your delivery by focusing on eye contact if you know you have a tendency to read your notes, or on eye contact and vocal variety if last time you spoke in a soft monotone; your practice time will be much more useful if you do not waste it trying to concentrate on your voice, eyes, posture, gestures, and presentational aids all in equal measure. This narrowing approach is also effective because you can manage anxiety by concentrating on your progress with something specific that you have chosen to improve. If last time you read your speaker's outline in a soft monotone, without looking at your audience, and you cannot change this entirely in your next speech, you can at least practice making consistent, broad eye contact. Accomplishing this goal will boost your confidence and may also have subtle and positive effects on how you use your voice over time.

Exercise 17D

1. Identify at least two specific ways you would like to grow as a speaker in terms of your delivery (use of voice, face, and/or body).

    Delivery Objectives

    _____

    _____

When and Where

You can prepare for effective practice by next identifying *when* and *where* you will practice. Recognize two important aspects of practice relating to time and space: You do not need to practice your entire speech each time you practice, and while practicing, you do not always need to be in a private space where you can stand up. Freeing yourself to practice within more flexible times and spaces can help you give yourself permission to practice more often and can also give you greater command in organizing your speech and its elements (as we discussed in the section about chunking).

When

Once you have divided your speech by completing the lists of speech segments and delivery goals above, you can set a specific amount of time for the *first pass* at each item on the list. No practice session should be shorter than 10 minutes, but you can allocate an amount of time for each item on the list based on the scope of the segment and how much time you have. Creating this kind of list helps you identify time because it prevents you from dismissing short sessions as "useless"; if you have only 15 minutes to practice, choose an item from the list that can be practiced in the amount of time you have right now. The list should be updated each time you practice an item; rather than crossing the item off the list, simply change its time allocation to reflect how much more work it needs before you feel comfortable with your progress in that area.

Exercise 17E

Content Segments   *Practice Time*

_____

_____

_____

_____

_____

_____

_____

Delivery Objectives   *Practice Time*

_____

_____

Where

A major advantage of the system described here is that you can find opportunities to practice apart from being in a private room. If you carry your full-sentence outline with you everywhere, can you practice a content segment while waiting for transportation? While something bakes in the oven? While your child takes a nap? If you work on only a single delivery objective while practicing your introduction, such as using your face to smile and respond expressively to what you say, can you do this while listening to music without words? Once you know the introduction well, can you practice this same delivery objective while driving?

Remember that you can also practice delivering your speech using the "Practice Timer" in SpeechPlanner (speechplanner.sagepub.com).

CHAPTER 18
Delivering Your Speech

If you envision your public speaking opportunities as dialogues with your audience, you can more effectively respond to these opportunities in resourceful ways—ways that turn your nervousness and anticipation into energy that moves and reshapes your body. While it is true that public speaking requires you to develop vocal and physical skills distinct from those people use in ordinary conversation, these skills are rooted in the responsiveness that pulls us, that tugs at us, when we engage others dialogically. Reflect on a recent successful, interesting, one-to-one or small-group oral interaction; perhaps you listened as a friend told an interesting story, or perhaps you convinced some family members to reconsider a suggestion you made. Was your gaze unfocused and withdrawn, or was it sharp and directed, indicating your curiosity and commitment? Was your body rigid and unmoving, or was it relaxed yet poised, indicating your confidence that the other person enjoyed your company and wanted you to share the space? Was your voice distant and emotionless, or were your pitch, volume, and tone fluid and dynamic, indicating your assured command of the ideas and language that mattered in the situation? We assume that in each case, the latter condition was true—you had curious eyes, a poised body, and a lively voice. In this chapter, we offer some strategies for embodying these same qualities in the often higher-stakes setting of the public speech.

Anticipation

Public speaking opportunities, for almost all public speakers, certainly feature heightened intensity that settles in the body in predictable ways. These physiological changes are the result of increased production of adrenaline, a hormone designed to enhance our ability to respond quickly when we find ourselves in risky situations. Our heart rate increases, our senses and nerves are physically more sensitive to stimuli, and our breaths become shorter and quicker. These physiological changes can be understood positively as our body marshaling resources to help us sharpen our focus when we anticipate speaking publicly. Anticipation is something we bring with us into all communication situations, as our goals, values, and perceptual lenses shape how we communicate. The form that anticipation takes, and the way it affects us, changes with each person and each communication context.

Scholarship on certain communication contexts that many of us experience as high stress, such as public speeches, suggests that for some speakers, the anxiety responses triggered might be quite difficult, if not impossible, to change permanently—even with careful training (McCroskey & Beatty, 1986). However, if we strive not to "overcome" anxiety-based responses but, rather, to understand them better and even regard them as aspects of ourselves that make us unique speakers, we can empower ourselves and one another to take responsibility for the special power effective public speakers can wield. We believe that, just as every person deserves respect as a participant in dialogue, every person—even those with significant anxiety responses in public speaking contexts—deserves the chance to influence others in the public sphere.

We believe that welcoming the physiological and psychological states that public speaking produces in our bodies can, if we treat these changes with respect and learn to work within them, enhance our public speaking effectiveness no matter what our intrinsic traits might be.

Focus

Training yourself to reflect commitment in a public speaking context requires attention to a much broader, deeper space than we experience in typical dialogical contexts. A common strategy speakers use to prepare for this context is called *visualization*, which involves carefully and precisely concentrating your mind, during practice, on your anticipated future speaking situation: Where are you standing? How are you standing? How many people are in the audience? How far away from you are the farthest listeners? How widely does the audience stretch, left to right, when viewed from your perspective? What are the first words you will say, and how will you say them? In the previous section, on *practice*, we offered some strategies for preparing your mind to speak confidently. Here, we center our attention on preparing your body—shifting the emphasis from you, the speaker, to your physical relationship to the audience.

For instance, a good way to help yourself develop focusing techniques appropriate for a public speaking context is to repeatedly practice, using visualization, addressing a much larger, more distant audience than the one for which you will actually speak. First, return to a dialogic setting, visualizing how important *eye contact* can be for establishing and maintaining a strong relationship with your dialogue partner. Eye contact expectations vary from culture to culture, but in many professional Western cultural contexts, we expect speakers to include all listeners with eye contact, to maintain eye contact for a few seconds, and then to break that eye contact for a moment or two before returning to it. Can you feel your shoulders and hips naturally move, in subtle ways, to maintain appropriate eye contact and keep that relationship physically strong if you visualize a one-to-one or small-group dialogue? Can you feel yourself occasionally complementing your words with gestures, even if you are not someone who tends to "talk with your hands"?

Next, begin visualizing your public speaking context. If your class of about 30 people will attend your speech, visualize a room of twice that number—rows of seats extended significantly farther, left and right, broadening your field of peripheral vision, with seats also extended twice as deep as your own classroom allows. How would an audience member to your extreme left feel included in your speech? How would an audience member in the very back of this visualized "double-sized" classroom feel included? How can you use your eyes, shoulders, and arms to reach out to the person seated to your extreme left, if you practice a portion of your speech a few times by imagining that this person is your most important audience member? Try practicing a few times again, with a different portion of your speech, by imagining that a single person in the very back of the room is your most important audience member. How can you use your eyes, shoulders, and arms to connect with that person? If your visualization during practice sessions includes this "double-sized" classroom on a consistent basis, you should find two useful benefits when you speak for your actual class: (1) You will find it easier to use eye contact, subtle shifts in your hips and shoulders, and natural, complementing gestures to relate to your audience—an audience much narrower in scope than the one you visualized. (2) You will find it easier to avoid the habit of delivering your speech only to your public speaking instructor. (Further, this advice can also be useful when you are not speaking before a captive audience of your peers, such as when speaking in a professional or community context.)

Exercise 18A

1. How many people are in your audience for a public speech? _____
2. How many rows wide is the room where you are speaking? _____ Double that number here: _____

3. How many rows deep is the room where you are speaking? _____ Double that number here: _____
4. How many times did you practice speaking to a room twice as wide? _____
5. How many times did you practice speaking to a room twice as deep? _____

Embodiment

Returning again to a successful dialogue you've had recently, did you find it easier to be attentive and focused when everyone involved was relaxed in their posture, yet also alert and aware? Most members of your audience will tend to mirror the ways you embody your speech; if your body, when speaking, is relaxed, confident, and focused, you will find an audience filled with people reflecting those qualities in their own bodies. The best way to gain greater and greater control of your posture and voice, as you develop your public speaking abilities, is to gain greater and greater control over your breathing. Remember that adrenaline will cause almost every person who takes the public speaking stage to take short, quick breaths—as if the speaker were about to sprint away from danger. You need not be governed by your natural adrenaline, however, if you use breathing techniques to practice breathing in the ways you wish. On your own time, not necessarily while doing "speaking practice," try concentrating on your breathing. If the context allows it, you can even do this in class, especially as you become more and more familiar with the process of concentrated breathing, because you'll get better and better at concentrating on your breathing while still focusing your mind on other tasks at the same time. How deeply do you draw in each breath? How long do you hold each breath before you exhale? Can you feel your diaphragm moving if you try? Can you feel how your diaphragm's contractions relate to the size and shape of the air cavity in your body? These answers will be different for each person, and each person will have a unique way of feeling her or his breath course through the body. What matters is that you become more fully conscious of the breathing process.

As you get better at concentrated breathing, try integrating it into your practice sessions while getting ready for your speech. Notice that if you can gain control of how deeply you breath and how long you hold your breaths, even while focusing your mind on other things, you can gain more control over your posture and muscle tension. Often, what makes a person who feels anxiety "look anxious" to others is the result of short, rapid breathing; this style of breathing makes the skin flush, the sweat glands activate, and the small muscles in the body twitch involuntarily—qualities we learn to read on other people as "anxiety." If you can become comfortable controlling the rate and depth of your breathing, making each public speaking context a trigger for you to breathe more slowly and deeply, your audience will read you as relaxed, confident, and even poised. And you will likely feel more relaxed, confident, and poised.

A further benefit of controlling your breathing relates to the section on *focus* above: When speaking in public, you need more than just eye contact and natural movement to establish and maintain a relationship with your audience; you also need a strong, audible voice. Projecting your voice across a room becomes much easier if you are breathing deeply and slowly, because you use your diaphragm not only to draw in air but also to forcefully push a column of air out to speak more loudly. When practicing, try making your voice louder without straining your vocal chords; focus only on simple vowel sounds (don't worry about using "real words," just practice the vowel sounds), and project them as loudly as you can without tiring your voice. Your vocal chords tire quickly; your diaphragm, a very strong muscle, does not. If you practice making louder and louder vowel sounds without tiring your voice, you will find that you have control, with the help of your diaphragm, over how loudly you can project your voice.

Exercise 18B

1. How many times did you concentrate on your breathing this week? _____

Voice

In addition to gaining control over the loudness of your voice (*dynamics*), you can also gain greater control over the gentle rise and fall of your vocal *pitch*. When we speak, most of us use pitch inflections (making the sound of a word or syllable higher or lower, as with a musical note) to demonstrate interest in and commitment to what we are saying. This is true in many cultures, even in stress-based languages such as English, where words have different meanings depending on which syllable is stressed; some languages, which are pitch based, feature even more frequent changes in pitch because words have different meanings based on the pitch used.

Another way we signal interest in and commitment to what we are saying is by varying *tone quality*, or the way we say words. Though each of us uses a range of tone qualities when we speak, the patterns of choices we make—the range of tone qualities—is different for each person, and is shaped by factors such as breathing style and other physiology, gender and family socialization, and personal history. When you think of a person you know well and whose voice you can immediately recognize, even out of context, such as a parent, what you are responding to is that person's tone quality.

Again, cultural variety means that pitch and tone variation happens less frequently in some cultures than in others. But in professional Western cultural contexts, many listeners expect each sentence to include some rise and fall in pitch and some subtle variation in tone, and these same listeners learn to associate speakers who lack pitch variety with a lack of interest or a lack of honesty. What this means to you as a speaker is that you should strive, when practicing, to listen to your own voice and learn to recognize how it sounds. This is one reason why working with a friend, or an audio-recording device, for some of your practice sessions can be helpful. Learn to recognize when your voice is more "flat," lacking in pitch or tone variety, compared with other portions of your speech. Do you have a tendency to speak more flatly when citing evidence? When offering signposts? When you are struggling to remember what you planned to say next? One goal in preparing yourself to speak well should be to identify where your own voice tends to flatten so you can give special attention to these moments and practice using vocal variety there, too. Avoid focusing on your entire speech this way, because you will nearly always find, if you attend to vocal variety carefully, that you naturally vary your voice at some points (introductions and conclusions are commonly characterized by greater vocal variety). "Natural" variety is your goal; so just attend, in practice, to those trouble spots.

Another way to give yourself greater opportunities to vary your tone and pitch is to *warm up* your voice before speaking. Many speakers and public performers use vocal exercises designed to make the lips, tongue, and vocal chords limber and responsive before taking the stage. The public speaking classroom does not always offer a chance to do this, because you will often be required to speak just after another person has finished. Ask your instructor if time can be made to do some vocal warm-up exercises at the start of class, or if speeches can be slotted in groups of three or four, with breaks between groups.

Reference

McCroskey, J. C., & Beatty, M. J. (1986). Oral communication apprehension. In W. H. Jones, J. M. Cheek, & S. R. Briggs (Eds.), *Shyness: Perspectives on research and treatment* (pp. 279–293). New York: Plenum Press.

CHAPTER 19

Reflection and Self-Assessment

As with any disciplined practice, effective public speaking will reward sustained reflection on your own efforts over time. Your public speaking instructor may provide you with structured assignments that require you to assess your speaking effectiveness. Here, we offer suggestions that can help you improve your speaking effectiveness by developing your own, personal reflection and assessment routine.

First, and most important, recognize that each public speech will, on reflection, include a mix of successes and learning opportunities. Even the most experienced and confident public speakers strive to learn from each speech. Second, these learning opportunities require you, the speaker, to make personal meaning from them. Your instructor, your classmates, and others in your life can help you by giving feedback that broadens your perspective, but you are the one who will need to integrate this feedback and your own impressions to become the person you will be when you next speak publicly.

Self-Assessment Materials

This means that the best way to develop your public speaking skills is to develop a process, meaningful for you, that allows you to systematically gather, retain, and learn from your public speaking experiences. Keeping a *journal* of some kind is an effective strategy for accomplishing these developmental goals and for preserving responses to your own speeches. Some speakers may prefer for this journal to be handwritten, because it is more personal; the process of writing by hand also can often trigger a unique conceptual link between hand and mind, allowing connections to surface that might not be so readily available with other forms of self-communication. Another way to generate a journal might be to use an audio-recording device; some speakers have day-to-day needs, such as frequent travel or frequent use of their hands, that prevent stable writing opportunities, but an audio-recording device can help fill this gap and ensure that you can document responses in a timely way. Finally, and perhaps most obviously, you can maintain a written electronic record of speaking responses in a digital file.

Some speakers prefer to document their actual speeches, using *video-recording* devices. Some instructors will require this in some classes. If you have access to a video recording of your speech, you have a strong advantage as you strive to develop as a public speaker because you can rely on concrete evidence of your efforts when making notes for the future. However, one disadvantage for some speakers when reviewing a video recording is intense self-criticism; most of us rarely see ourselves speak and act in day-to-day settings, and so we experience a powerful sense of alienation when we view ourselves in a video recording. This can lead to an impulse toward intense, negative self-criticism. If you are required, or choose, to view video recordings of yourself as a public speaker, keep the balance of these advantages and disadvantages in mind when you do so.

Exercise 19A

Self-Assessment Questions

Whether or not you choose to keep a permanent public speaking journal, and whether or not you choose to view video recordings of yourself speaking publicly, you can use some questioning techniques to reflect on your public speaking opportunities and integrate them into your life as a communicator. As you ask and answer the following questions, keep in mind that the advice we offer in Chapter 6, especially regarding being supportive rather than destructive and precise rather than vague, applies when responding to your own work as well. After each occasion on which you offer a public speech, try to document your responses to these questions as soon as you are able.

1. Why did I choose to speak? Was this an assignment? Was I representing my own interests and points of view or those of someone else? How much control did I have over the decision to speak?

   _____

   _____

   _____

   _____

   _____

   _____

2. What are my initial impressions of my own speech? What words would I choose to describe my speech to someone I trust but who did not see me speak, such as a family member or friend?

   _____

   _____

   _____

   _____

   _____

   _____

3. What were my goals as a speaker heading into this speech? Did I want to make sure I fit the time limit? Did I want a high grade? Did I have specific goals for improving from the last time I spoke?

   _____

   _____

_____

_____

_____

_____

_____

4. What are three specific successes from this speech, three specific things I did well?

_____

_____

_____

_____

_____

_____

_____

5. Which of the things I did well, listed in Question 4, relate directly to the goals I discussed in Question 3? Which did not? Am I surprised in any way by what I did well, and if so, why?

_____

_____

_____

_____

_____

_____

_____

6. What feedback did I receive about this speech? Did I receive immediate feedback in the situation? Did I receive feedback from my instructor? What were the focal points of this feedback, and how were these focal points like, or unlike, my listing of goals (Question 3) and successes (Question 4)?

_____

_____

_____

_____

_____

_____

_____

7. What three things about this speech do I choose to improve on the next time I speak publicly? Which of these come from my own goals and which from others' feedback?

_____

_____

_____

_____

_____

_____

_____

ⓢSAGE research**methods**

The essential online tool for researchers from the world's leading methods publisher

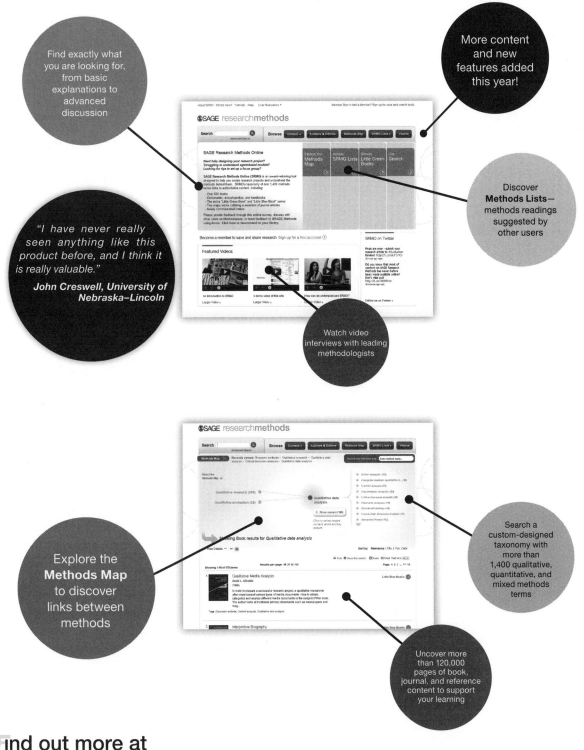

Find exactly what you are looking for, from basic explanations to advanced discussion

More content and new features added this year!

Discover **Methods Lists**— methods readings suggested by other users

"I have never really seen anything like this product before, and I think it is really valuable."

John Creswell, University of Nebraska–Lincoln

Watch video interviews with leading methodologists

Explore the **Methods Map** to discover links between methods

Search a custom-designed taxonomy with more than 1,400 qualitative, quantitative, and mixed methods terms

Uncover more than 120,000 pages of book, journal, and reference content to support your learning

Find out more at
www.sageresearchmethods.com